The Art of the Renaissance
in Northern Europe

LONDON : GEOFFREY CUMBERLEGE
OXFORD UNIVERSITY PRESS

The Art of
The Renaissance
in Northern Europe

ITS RELATION TO THE CONTEMPORARY SPIRITUAL
AND INTELLECTUAL MOVEMENTS

BY OTTO BENESCH

HARVARD UNIVERSITY PRESS

Cambridge, Massachusetts

1947

To
Zechariah Chafee, Jr.

Preface

THE CONTENT of this book was first presented to the public in a series of lectures delivered at the Lowell Institute in Boston in March 1944. The author wishes to express his thanks to the Trustees of the Lowell Institute, and also to Professor J. Douglas Bush. He feels particularly indebted to Dr. Arthur Burkhard for having revised the language of the text of the lectures.

For publication, the text has been enlarged and provided with notes. The author is indebted to the library of the Fogg Museum of Art, to Widener Library and Houghton Library of Harvard University, to the Boston Public Library, and to the Print Room of the Museum of Fine Arts, Boston, for the use of books and photographs needed for the illustrations.

Most valuable to the author was the advice and criticism given him by Professor Zechariah Chafee, Jr., when he had the privilege of discussing the text with him before its revision for publication. May he accept this book as a token of the author's gratitude.

O. B.

Fogg Museum of Art
July 1945

Contents

Illustrations

FIGURE

FIGURE

Text Figures

The Art of the Renaissance
in Northern Europe

Introduction

GREAT WORKS of art of the past are to us inexhaustible sources of enjoyment and elevation. Therefore, we are too readily inclined to consider them as creations of a timeless realm of absolute beauty, disconnected from the worries and troubles, from the torment and aspirations of a struggling human world. If we consider the foremost works of the artists of our era, we realize how much the deep split of our time, its anxieties and catastrophes are not only mirrored but even foreshadowed in the representational arts of the late nineteenth and twentieth centuries. It was not different in other centuries. Art has always been a function of human life, perhaps the most comprehensive and universal besides theoretical thinking. Therefore, it is a key to the understanding of the totality of life. On the other hand, the knowledge of the leading spiritual and intellectual movements of an era will help us to approach its artistic creations and illuminate the meaning of phenomena which appear strange and obscure because of remoteness of time. This applies especially to eras which were filled with great revolutions of the mind, with cataclysms and the rise of new worlds both in a literal and in a metaphorical sense, of eras which were as pregnant with new constructive and destructive forces as our own time. Such an era was the sixteenth century. Its splits and cleavages, its creative and conflicting trends, were not inferior to those of the twentieth century. The predominance of the fine arts in the imposing movement of the renascence in Italy lends to that particular chapter a unified aspect which is missing in Northern Europe. Nowhere did the artistic ideas stand so much in the foreground as in Italy. The picture which art offers in Germany and in the Netherlands, in France and England during that era, is a much more problematic and complex one. It demands a different method of approach. If our analysis should discuss only form and color, it would elude our efforts.

Such is the general problem and the task of these investigations. They do not attempt to give a panorama of all the overwhelming

richness of the era in concern.[1] They deal with selected problems
of the history of art, which are representative enough to give an
idea of the tremendous totality in question. They start from the
proper questions which concern the historian of art, and try to
find an answer to them by penetrating to the essentials of the
artistic facts which found their expression in different, yet genu-
inely related, forms in other fields of the creative human spirit as
well. The history of art is mainly the history of the artistic problems. As solutions of these problems could be found only by creative geniuses endowed with a vivid feeling for the totality of the
spiritual and human situation of their time, the understanding of
them presupposes the understanding of the aforementioned totality. Therefore, the method on which the present investigations
are based is that of the history of ideas as it was adapted to the
history of art by Max Dvořák and further developed. The author
gratefully professes himself as his pupil. These investigations owe
much to the teaching and work of Max Dvořák.

The great Austrian scholar of Czech descent first developed his
method and ideas in his work *Idealismus und Naturalismus in der
gotischen Skulptur und Malerei*, which grew out of his academic
lectures given at the University of Vienna.[2] Its continuation was
laid down in academic lecture courses given during the years 1915
to 1917 under the titles "Idealismus und Realismus in der Kunst
der Neuzeit" and "Ueber das Verhältnis der Kunst des 17. und
18. Jahrhunderts zu den gleichzeitigen geistigen Strömungen."
The latter course brought the synthesis and final formulation of
Dvořák's new approach to the problems of art and spirit of the past.

From his newly won standpoint, Dvořák reconsidered the problems of Italian art of the Renaissance in his academic lectures during the winters of the years 1918 to 1920.[3] His early death in 1921
prevented him from carrying through systematically the same
work for the field of the Renaissance in Northern Europe. Yet
the project must have been in his mind, as is testified by important
beginnings in his course "Idealismus und Realismus in der Kunst
der Neuzeit" and in single essays on Schongauer, Dürer, Bruegel,
and El Greco.

The present investigations attempt to proceed on ways opened
by Max Dvořák as a pioneer. The ideas expounded in them have

been most strongly fostered through the author's research work in the Albertina, that unique treasure house of cultural history laid down in printed art and drawings.

The history of art at the present owes more to Max Dvořák than is generally admitted. In developing his new method, he was often inspired by the achievements brought about in the fields of the history of religion, philosophy, and literature by Wilhelm Dilthey and Ernst Troeltsch.

Today, the methodical urge to extend the history of ideas to the field of the natural sciences is growing. Here the art historian also may gain new points of view.

I

The Medieval Heritage and the
New Empiricism

DURING the fifteenth century, when art in Italy was aiming
at a new secular and scientific understanding of the
physical world and when art in the Netherlands was
striving for a new interpretation of its visual beauty in the pious
mood of a still-medieval religiosity, edification and education completely overshadowed all self-consistent artistic problems in Central Europe. There scientific or exclusively artistic problems
meant little to the artists. Their works were intended to narrate
and to teach. It is not without significance that book printing and
the graphic arts were German inventions, that they found their
most extensive development in Central Europe and there engaged
the foremost artistic energies.[1]

Of course, during the fifteenth century, the artists of Germany, Bohemia, Switzerland, and Austria very ardently followed
up artistic problems as well — for instance the pictorial realization of solids, and of space as the result of their interrelation.
In the 1440's, we see this very clearly in the paintings of Conrad
Witz. We notice violent efforts to conquer a new kind of reality,
to achieve a new kind of plastic illusion. Yet the artist did not
regard his purpose as reached through that achievement, as an
Italian master would have done; his final aim was to give to an old
religious content a new intensity and nearness to life. In Italy, the
emphasis was greatly shifted from the old medieval stock of contents to new humanistic concepts. In Northern Europe, the old
contents kept their central position. Humanistic subjects, if they
penetrated from the South, were represented with a definitely
medieval flavor.[2] Thus the medieval spirit remained in power in
the North much longer than in the South, and it ruled the Ger-
manic countries especially in unbroken strength throughout the

major part of the fifteenth century, which in Italy at the very
beginning brought about the rise of a new humanism, a new
science, and a new grammar of artistic forms.

The era about 1500 was most prolific in great figures of European culture, mainly in the fields of art and religious thought.
If in history a wave of outstanding personalities coincides with
the daybreak of a new era of thought, the result is a spectacle of
overwhelming richness to the eyes of the student. Immense inner
tension finds its expression in meteoric creations and catastrophic
outbursts. Two worlds struggle with each other, and while the
stability of the one breaks down, the rise of the other unlooses
fluctuating forces. Tremendous new possibilities open, but do not
yet permit the crystallization of new norms. Everything appears
problematic in the twilight of dawn and dusk, through which the
creative spirits find their own way. This was the situation in
Germany at the end of the fifteenth and the beginning of the
sixteenth century. Out of its twilight, almost as a symbol of the
time, rises the figure of the most representative German artist,
Albrecht Dürer.

Dürer wrote down the most noteworthy events and facts con-
cerning his family in a memorial book.[3] His feeling for his family
and his devotion to his parents were almost religious. They were
different from that sponsorship of their own kindred which we
notice in the great Italian masters like Michelangelo and Titian.
They were deeply rooted in the medieval structure of society
based on religious notions, for which the painful earthly life is
only a transitory stage to a happier beyond. After having described the death of his mother, he adds: "God the Lord grant me
that I too may attain a happy end, and that God with his heavenly
host, my father, mother, relations, and friends may come to my
death. And may God Almighty give unto us eternal life. Amen."
Here the words of the master conjure up a picture of the last hour
quite common to late medieval imagery. A South German woodcut from about 1400 represents the death of the Virgin in this way,
with Christ and saintly figures from the beyond intermingling with
the Apostles still dwelling on earth to assist His Holy Mother in her
last hour.[4] A host of sacred persons, in whom heaven and earth
are blended into a spiritual unity, who follow in the soft, melodious

flow of their forms an ideal of spiritual beauty, crowd around the dying Virgin. In a similar way, a woodcut of the Late Gothic block-book entitled *Ars moriendi*[5] shows a throng of visitors from the beyond surrounding the bed of a dying man, chasing away the demons and receiving him into their celestial community. This illustrated book, which was made in the Netherlands about 1460, taught men the art of dying happily, of overcoming the last afflictions and winning eternal bliss. It was copied repeatedly in Germany, and its moral idea certainly engendered Dürer's prayer from an anxious heart. If we read Dürer's characterization of his parents in the memorial book, we find a faithful and moving portrayal of those people who lived their lives between the narrow walls of a gloomy German city, girdled with bastions, rising to the sky with pointed spires, roofs, and gables. They clung to the tradition of their medieval world, which they did not replace by new buildings, as Machiavelli noted with surprise in 1508. Modest, parsimonious, righteous, socially oppressed bourgeois, they prepared themselves for a better after-world. This earthly world was a transitory one to them; their society with its ranks was a stair to heaven administered by the church, as Thomas Aquinas and the medieval thinkers taught.

And yet a human immediacy which goes far beyond the tone of medieval chronicles is shown by Dürer's description of the last hour of his mother:

> She often had the plague and many other severe and strange illnesses, and she suffered great poverty, scorn, contempt, mocking words, terrors, and great adversities. Yet she bore no malice! . . . She feared Death much, but she said that to come before God she feared not. Also she died hard, and I marked that she saw something dreadful, for she asked for the holy-water, although for a long time she had not spoken. Immediately afterwards, her eyes closed over. I saw also how Death smote her two great strokes to the heart, and how she closed mouth and eyes and departed with pain. I repeated to her the prayers. I felt so grieved for her that I cannot express it. . . .

These words read as if they were written by a great modern writer, and although the suggestion that the woman saw "something dreadful" recalls the incarnate demonry of the images, the last pitiful struggle of a poor human being is described so directly that it brings to our eyes the great charcoal drawing (Fig. 2) which the master made of his mother shortly before her death in 1514.[6] It has a merciless, almost cruel, veracity. Barbara Dürer, aged before her time, emaciated by the harshness of life and by sickness, looks like a skeleton, all skin and bones, sad, burned out, yet full of a tremendous acquiescence in God. The lines, as realistic as possible, lend to the almost life-sized head an expressive grandeur beyond compare. In this portrait there speaks an immediate experience of life, directly human, unbroken by dogma and ecclesiastic teaching. A new notion of freedom and reality stands out from the gloomy medieval background, victorious even in the sight of death.

The time in which Dürer lived was full of anxieties, marked with that tension which accompanies the tides of great eras of human thought. Miraculous phenomena and appearances seemed to forbode portentous things and filled the people with awe. Dürer himself regarded them with the naïve belief of the medieval man in miracles. "The greatest miracle which I ever have seen happened in the year 1503, when crosses rained down on many people, on children more than on other people. Among those crosses I saw one as I have drawn it here." The nebulous shape of a crucifixion had fallen on the linen shirt of a little maid, who was deeply distressed, as the painter adds. He further mentions that he saw a comet in the sky, like the one he engraved in the background, of his famous "Melancholy." The mood of chiliasm, of the end of the world, pervaded the time about the year 1500 just as it filled the time about the year 1000. In those days, people turned to the prophecies of former ages, which came to have a new and actual meaning for them. This is the spiritual background of the greatest work of the young Dürer, the illustrations for the Apocalypse, the Revelation of St. John the Divine, done in the last years of the fifteenth century.[7] The aforementioned phenomena in nature must have evoked imaginings in Dürer similar to those described in chapter VI of the Revelation: "And the sun became black as sackcloth of hair, and the moon became red as blood; and the stars of heaven fell unto the earth." In Dürer's woodcut the hail of star-shaped flames pours down on mankind vainly trying to hide in cliffs — emperor and pope, peasant and beggar alike. The sky rolls up like a scroll and the rocks totter. The voluminous figures in the foreground are frightening in their distress and helplessness, as the fiery disaster rains down on them from the sky. The cosmic scene, in its fusing of heaven and earth into one great unity, is indebted to the abstract compositions of the Middle Ages which represent supernatural catastrophes, yet it breaks up their orderliness into a reeling chaos of harshly conflicting, expressive shapes. The medieval world structure is still there, but it is beginning to crack and to stagger.

Thus Dürer imagined the downfall of the universe in the last years of the old century, when he was still linked up with the thinking of medieval eschatology. Let us compare with the illustrations to the Apocalypse just described a most revealing dream vision of the Last Day which he had in 1525, three years before his death. Dürer's impressible, vivid fantasy was prolific in dreams. Once he observed to his friends that in his dreams he often saw works of art of such beauty that if they were reality he would be the happiest man on earth. Yet his dream world produced not only beautiful things but also the horrors feared by a pious mind, living under the tension and anxieties of the time. He was so deeply stirred by the dream vision of 1525 that he painted it in water colors (Fig. 5) and provided it with the following inscription:

In the night between Wednesday and Thursday, after Whitsunday, I saw this appearance in my sleep — how many great waters fell from heaven. The first struck the earth about four miles away from me with terrific force and tremendous noise, and it broke up and drowned the whole land. I was so sore afraid that I awoke from it. Then the other waters fell, and as they fell they were very powerful and there were many of them, some further away, some nearer. And they came down from so great a height that they all seemed to fall with an equal slowness. But when the first water that touched the earth had very nearly reached it, it fell with such swiftness, with wind and roaring, and I was so sore afraid that when I awoke my whole body trembled and for a long while I could not recover myself. So when I arose in the morning I painted it above here as I saw it. God turn all things to the best.[8]

This vision is of a very different kind from the transcendental religious imaginings of the earlier years. In spite of its cosmic grandeur, it is based on experience of reality. An immense plain stretches before us, with towns and cities minute in their remoteness. The impression we receive is that the surface of the earth forms a wide vault. The whole is seen from the standpoint of an individual, subjective onlooker, lost in this immense width of space beneath the dome of the sky and terrified by the phenomenon. The waters roaring down have a deep blue color, the waterspouts become lighter in the distance, the farther back in space they fall. This view is the perception of an eye trained by physical experience and accustomed to building up a notion of reality from empirical facts. The real relations and distances are accurately observed and estimated, and combined by a calculating mind into a rational notion of space.

This calculating mind reached its climax in Dürer's theoretical writings, to which the master gave so much care during his last years: The Instruction in the Mensuration with Compass and Triangle (1525),[9] The Theory of Fortification (1527),[10] and the Four Books on Human Proportion, most important to the artist, but not published until after his death.[11] They combine the practical experiences of many years of working, thinking, investigating — all that newly won treasure of artistic empiricism which the new era had made possible. It is a rational synthesis, such as Leonardo da Vinci had in mind without ever achieving its literary completion. Dürer's literary projects also remained partly fragments. He planned a comprehensive book on the theory and practice of art, of which there are drafts interspersed with specimens of another handwriting.[12] Dürer often accepted the help of his humanistic friends in the literary formulation of ideas which were either his own or adopted by him. He corresponded with Niklas Kratzer, mathematician and astronomer at the English court. We read in the London manuscripts the following sentences: "There is no art by which Measurement is more, and more variously, needed than the Art of Painting, which not only requires Geometry and Arithmetic, the foundations of all Measurement, but, much more than any other art, depends upon Perspective, Catoptrica, Geodaesia, Chorographia." A late woodcut by Dürer, representing the siege of a fortress (Fig. 6), is assumed to have been projected as an illustration for the Theory of Fortification, although it was published as a single woodcut. If we look at the immense maplike panorama of a plain with an army drawn up before a fortified city, while villages burn on the horizon, we understand the penetration of Dürer's concept of nature by a rational intellect, a development which took place in his later years. This same rational mind, supported by empirical knowledge, mastered the illusion of space in the water color of the deluge and made it different from the cosmic catastrophes delineated in the Apocalypse — nearer to nature, and thus even more oppressive and ominous.

This empiricism was a conquest which Northern European art owes to Dürer, a conquest to which sudden, lightning perceptions and tenacious systematic study equally contributed. Both forms of conquering the empirical world are noted in the art of Dürer — the former mainly in his drawings, the latter mainly in his theoretical studies. They correspond to the two foremost intellectual trends of Dürer's era, the intuitive and the didactic. Artistic intuition had as large a share in the intellectual achievements of the Renaissance as the tendency to bring all knowledge into teachable and scholarly transmittable form.

Although the new empiricism finally came to be the strongest force to rise against the medieval convention and tradition, its roots were already contained in the stone-carved universe of the Gothic cathedral with its marvelous observations of plants and realistic studies of human faces and their expressions. As often happens in history, the force which was to become the impetus of a new era grew up in the shadow of the old one. Many of Leonardo's revolutionizing ideas were derived from Nicolaus Cusanus' late medieval philosophical system.[13] Thus the roots of this empiricism are apparent in Dürer's very beginnings. They were implanted in him as a part of the medieval heritage which he received from the Late Gothic masters. They gradually transformed and destroyed that heritage, and developed into a completely new notion of the visible world.

In the dedication of the Instruction in the Mensuration to his closest friend, the humanist Willibald Pirckheimer, Dürer wrote the following:

Until now, many talented boys in Germany were raised as painters, instructed without any reason and merely by daily habit. They grew up like wild, ungrafted trees. Although some of them through constant practice acquired a free hand, so that they formed their works mightily, yet unconsiderately and arbitrarily, reasonable painters have scorned their blindness. It is evident that the German painters with their able hand and practice of color have acquired no little skill, yet they lack the art of measuring.

What Dürer meant by those artists who grew up like "ungrafted trees" and achieved "mighty works" becomes clear if we look at the works of his own youth. A drawing of the Crucifixion in the Louvre (Fig. 1), done about 1489,[14] is a work much in the line of the altar panels which were produced in the shop of his master Michael Wolgemut in the 1480's, when the boy Dürer was an apprentice there. It contains nothing of the great, monumental simplicity of the late Dürer. It is of pictorial richness, filled with restless, creeping, curling, flickering lines, crammed with various motives in the background. The forms are lean, brittle, full of expressive motions. The figures are entangled with the landscape; the profusion of characteristic details results in an unclear totality. These are features of an era coming to its end, the era of the Late Gothic, in the tradition of which the young Dürer grew up.[15] The works of the great painter and engraver Martin Schongauer of Colmar in Alsace, to visit whom Dürer left his native city and traveled as a journeyman to the Upper Rhine, are basically no different. They are more elegant and precise, superior in quality to the wooden and morose panels of Nuremberg, and make better use of the courtly mode of the Netherlanders, yet they cultivate the interlaced, restless, spiny and brittle style to the utmost refinement. Here we clearly observe that a great artistic tradition is dying away, the tradition of Gothic art.

Dürer's stay away from home was much protracted; it lasted from 1490 to 1494. Although he found Schongauer no longer alive when he arrived in Colmar, the journey was of the greatest advantage in his development because it brought him into the very centers of book printing, illustrating, and publishing, which were also centers of the graphic arts. He found plenty of work in the printing offices of Basel and Strassburg. These places were also centers of the intellectual life of the time, storehouses of medieval thought and poetry, yet already open to the messages of ancient and Renaissance humanism which began to dawn from the South. Through the channels of writing and publishing it came to the North, which first dealt with it in a late medieval way, because it took years for the fine arts to follow literature.

In 1492, the publisher Kessler in Basel brought out a Latin edition of the epistles of St. Jerome which Dürer adorned with a woodcut representing the Saint caring for the wounded paw of his lion.[16] It has a rough grandeur in its towering medieval shape, in the Gothic obliqueness of its space construction; it is formed impressively and "mightily," like the works of those wild-grown young painters of whom Dürer later wrote. Dürer apparently was successful with it because he received commissions for other illustrations. Some of these are still debated by the Dürer specialists, but his style is evident in certain of the illustrations for books of secular content including an educational work entitled "The Knight of the Tower";[17] the comedies of Terence, which never progressed beyond a preparatory stage; and Sebastian Brant's *Ship of Fools*.[18]

In literature Sebastian Brant represents a critical and sceptical trend of thought which began to question and to doubt the old moral and social order. Brant did this book in a vein of mockery which essentially is related to the scurrilous grotesques playing their games in the labyrinths of ornamentation in Gothic capitals, boltels, choir stalls, and book pages. Those grotesques acquired self-sufficient life in the works of the German engravers and of that greatest genius among all mockers, the Dutch painter Hieronymus Bosch. In Brant's *Ship of Fools* they hold up a mirror to the queerness of human life. To ridicule it is the best way to denounce it. The jester was allowed to utter things which the preacher could not risk. Savonarola was burnt at the stake, while nobody interfered with Brant's book. The *Ship of Fools* cruises through all latitudes of human society, and illuminates many dark corners of clerical and secular life. The hypocritic monk receives his due as well as the young fool who for money's sake marries an old woman. Social criticism on the eve of the Reformation was possible under the protection of the fool's cap. Dürer took part in the illustration of this book, which appeared in 1494. It required from a young artist not only vivid imagination but also sharp observation to illustrate such profane subjects.

The keenness of his observation appears in a self-portrait which the young artist sketched with the pen on his journey (Fig. 9). These dark brooding eyes pierce reality, seize it with tremendous earnestness. The journeyman portrayed here was struggling with the empirical world, endeavoring to formulate it in a new vision. It was a daring and bold enterprise for a German artist of the fifteenth century to show his own image faithfully in such a rhapsodic way. Drawing was to the young Dürer a new means of conquering the visible world, not in the slow and considerate method of the Gothic designer, but in the glow and inspiration of the moment, stimulated by a vivid perception. A new type of drawing came about in this way.

Medieval drawing looked very different. The French architect Villard d'Honnecourt, who worked in the thirteenth century at the cathedral of Cambrai, collected in a travel sketchbook all kinds of motifs valuable for a medieval artist. One of its pages shows motion and proportion studies of human figures, reduced to geometrical diagrams which are derived from abstract mathematical concepts, the same concepts which rule the transcendental geometry of the High Gothic cathedral.[19] The things are not given with reality, but expressed through geometrical tokens. We may compare this intellectual procedure with a trend in the nominalistic medieval philosophy, mainly connected with William of Occam. It is called terminism, because it expresses the reality of things through intuitive notions of them, which serve as signs (*termini*) to identify them, without having a factual similarity to them. How much Dürer's art replaces the sign by the thing itself becomes evident in the many sketches in which he seizes upon the nearest things surrounding him: pieces of drapery, garments, cushions, his own left hand,[20] and even his own left leg.[21] This realism was no contradiction to the medieval concept, which permitted a continually progressing study of nature within the framework of the religious and feudal totality. Late medieval art increasingly shows features which we call "genre." The graphic arts especially excelled in them. One of Dürer's finest precursors, the Master of the Housebook, represents in his delicate drypoints charming scenes from everyday life. Dürer followed his footsteps when he drew himself leading a pretty girl of Basel to a dance, both dressed according to the newest fashion.[22] We miss in Dürer's pen drawing the Late Gothic grace and delicacy of the Housebook Master's work, yet there is instead of that a new powerful sense of reality which was of greater importance for the future.

We would be wrong to assume that a German Renaissance art came about merely through casual contact between the art of the South and the North, causing a transformative influence of the former on the latter. Northern art had to mature by itself to the point where it could turn voluntarily to the South. When Dürer made his first journey to Venice in 1495–96, his main psychological reason — besides the particular reason to escape the plague at home — was to widen his spiritual horizon, to open his eyes to overwhelming new impressions. His purpose was to discover new worlds, to gain experience through empirical contact, which no artist of his narrow Gothic native city had gained before. We find him copying Italian engravings, playing cards, and costume drawings. But that he could have done in Germany before. The new element was not so much the art with which he made contact in Italy; basically, he remained in the Late Gothic tradition. The new element was the different spirit, the different attitude of life which he experienced, the different atmosphere which he breathed. The tension, the striving for great yet unknown things, found a solution. The magnificent flow of the brush draws the vigorous and graceful figure of a female nude on the light surface of the paper, studied from life, full of freshness and elasticity.[23] It conveys a new idea of the human being as a living organism, foreign to Dürer before.

The journey was no less important than the stay in the artistic metropolis itself. For the first time in his life, Dürer experienced the spell of the high mountains when he crossed through the valleys of the Tyrol. The surface of the world structure rolls in great waves of cosmic rhythm, towers up to snowy peaks, sinks down in the depth of the valleys.[24] We stand before a new fact: man as a lonely being in the scenery overwhelmed by its grandeur pours his joy and devotion into a work which serves no other purpose than to give expression to this feeling of discovery and adventure in a new world. The wide circular valley of Trent opens up (Fig. 7), surrounded by rock walls which shimmer in a mirage-like blue, amethyst-violet and rose.[25] They are inflamed by the morning sun which climbs over the ridges. The defiant walls of the somber old town float between the silver mirror of the river and the rising morning mist.

The only parallels which can be found to these amazing works are the studies which Leonardo da Vinci made in the Alps surrounding Lombardy and Piedmont. While Leonardo tried to explore the tectonics of the mountains in the spirit of scientific objectivity, Dürer was spellbound by those less tangible values, color, atmosphere, and mood. We sense a spring morning in the mountains. The French and Netherlandish book illuminators had broken the way to the representation of such phenomena; yet never before Dürer did these phenomena give rise to a work of art in its own right. His eyes once opened, Dürer discovered similar novelties in his native surroundings. A water color preserved in London [26] depicts a sunrise in the pine woods near Nuremberg. The atmospheric spectacle dominates all picturesque wealth of form, even disrupts the solemn rhythm of the high forest. The painter's eye clings spellbound to the zones of fiery red, flaming golden yellow and orange which fan out between a fringe of blackish blue clouds. It is the expressive spirit of landscape which fascinated Dürer here even more than its objective tectonics.

Leonardo's scientific attitude towards nature was largely influenced by the philosophical doctrine and the teachings of the German thinker Nicolaus Cusanus, who was bishop of Brixen in Tyrol. This last great philosopher of the Middle Ages attempted to harmonize the growing trend to empirical investigation with the great old religious world concept.[27] He established the notions of the finite and the infinite which are united in one great harmony. God, the infinite, is contained in every little thing, which therefore deserves our attention. Every small part reflects the cosmos, becomes a mirror of the universe — "in omnibus partibus relucet totum" — as in Dürer's Sunrise every inch of the awakening forest seems to pulsate in the rhythm of the universe. Cusanus' philosophy contributed more than any other to the breaking up of the medieval system, which he thought to preserve. Older than the painters, intellectually he broke open the way to a concept of nature, which the fine arts first realized in full.

When Dürer sketched this marvelous water color, he was working on the greatest enterprise of his youth, the Apocalypse. The task as such forms a great contrast to the world of reality which he had just discovered. The Apocalypse is a feverish vision of horrid happenings and cosmic catastrophes, proclaimed by a revenging God. It was written in the time of the religious and racial persecutions under the Emperor Nero. Its gloomy, tremendously expressive imaginings seem to defy all artistic visualization, and to be accessible only to an abstract, symbolical representation, appropriate to medieval art. Apocalyptic subjects had played a great part in the iconographical program since the early Middle Ages. They filled the portals and stained glass windows of the cathedrals. A German manuscript from St. Stephen's at Bamberg, written in the era of the Saxon Emperor Henry II, about 1007, illustrates the Apocalypse in a mood of gloomy, abstract monumentality.[28] The eighteenth chapter describes the destruction of Babylon through fire falling from heaven. The ships move from the harbor and the sailors, watching the disaster, try to save their lives, as thousands have done in our time in the burning cities of Europe. "And a mighty angel took up a stone like a great millstone, and cast it into the sea, saying, Thus with violence shall that great city of Babylon be thrown down, and shall be found no more at all." The early medieval miniature shows a majestic, somber angel striding over the waves in a pattern-like ideal space. He becomes tremendous through his loneliness in the vast, empty field of gold and rose, which his jagged silhouette dominates. His act of destruction, of submerging the millstone, is like a solemn ritual. Dürer's woodcuts, on the other hand, are full of uproar. One of them (Fig. 3) illustrates chapters VIII and IX — the sounding of the seven trumpets and the destruction of the earth. Dürer had to deal with visions which accepted life in the glowing, metaphoric language of the religious visionary but seemed to defy the pencil of the artist. The medieval artist expressed them through great symbols in timeless surroundings. Dürer, too, necessarily brought this universality and timelessness into his work. The composition rises like a steep wall into the space of the universe. Heaven and earth fuse into one great unit. Yet all the experience of reality which he had gained in the meanwhile could not be eliminated. It was Dürer's immense achievement that his strength of imagination and mastery of the real were able to incorporate and give convincing shape to those gigantic visions conjured up in an ecstatic language. This has nothing to do with Italian influence.

In some of the virile angels' noble features we may sense an echo of Mantegna's valiant warriors. But this is not the decisive factor. The decisive factor is the new spirit of reality which pervades the whole. Dürer's illustration is literal and more realistic than any earlier. We *see* the hail of fire mingled with blood which pours down from the first trumpet; the great mountain burning with fire which was cast into the sea at the sound of the second trumpet; the star which fell on the fountain at the sound of the third trumpet. The voice, which cries "Woe," dashes from the clouds as a bird of prey, and sun and moon shrink visibly, struggling with the night. Here Dürer spreads the universe before us like a huge cosmography, like one of those maps in sixteenth-century prints which try to portray the surface of the globe or the starry sky. All this reality only increases the visionary character. It is a dreamlike reality, appropriate to the sight of the Evangelist who "immediately was in the spirit." If we compare a celestial scene in the *Schatzbehalter* of Dürer's master Wolgemut,[29] Christ with the tools of the Passion kneeling before God the Father, it looks almost banal in its everyday naturalism beside Dürer's overwhelming vision. Dürer's work has more affinity to the visionary Evangelists in the Gospels of Otto III, a work of the school of Reichenau [30] done about the year 1000 in a time of similar tension, full of dark forebodings. Is what we see in Dürer's Apocalypse a survival of the Middle Ages? It would be better to call it a revival of that great and heroic spirit of the early and high Middle Ages, which had long been lost in the narrow bourgeois world of the Late Gothic.

How Dürer was inspired by visions of past ages of Christianity is shown to us in the solemn altar panel of All Saints who adore the Trinity in the shape of the Throne of Mercy (Fig. 8). Dürer painted it in 1511 for the little chapel of an asylum for twelve aged poor men which was founded by the pious Matthäus Landauer. It radiated in the rainbow splendor of its colors on the altar. The community of All Saints kneel in the celestial spheres offering their prayers to the Trinity; beneath them is the huge circle of the faithful, the visible church, reëchoed in the highest spheres by hosts of angels. All ranks of society are represented, from Pope and Emperor to burgher and peasant. A cardinal invites the humble old donor to join. As Erwin Panofsky in his exhaustive interpretation of the content first has shown, the painting represents the community of the faithful, the City of God of St. Augustine, who contemplate God in eternity.[31] "Wherefore it may be, and it is very credible, that then we shall so see the worldly bodies of the new heaven, and new earth, as we see God present everywhere." The crowd of figures floating above our eye level extends into an unsurveyable depth, mastered with all knowledge of scientific perspective. The cloud on which they rest extends far beyond the horizon of the enchanting earthly paradise on the lower margin, although their brocades drag down to a point even nearer than the little figure of the modest yet proud painter in the lower right corner. Thus, they grow into the superhuman, and all mastery of nature serves the purpose of visualizing the supernatural.

The peculiarity of Dürer which some scholars have called his "curiosity" is the eagerness with which he absorbed all the large and small miracles produced by nature, either in his native surroundings or abroad. There was nothing so insignificant that he would not have considered it as worthy of representation. In the first years of the sixteenth century and during his journey to the Netherlands (1520–21), especially, we notice an increase of studies from nature. He dug out a patch of grassy ground with the most common native herbs and flowers, and devoted to it one of his most magnificent water colors, in which the tender sprouting stalks and panicles rise with the grandeur of a solemn edifice.[32] A similar water color he devoted to one of the denizens of that vegetable world, a young field hare.[33] The animal is portrayed not only to the most minute detail of its fluffy fur but also in its shy and apprehensive character, ready to jump away at any moment, although it had to pose in the master's studio, as is indicated by the reflection of the cross-bar of the window in the sparkling pupil of its eye. While Dürer stayed in the Netherlands he collected all kinds of rare animals, plants, and fruits. He traveled to Zeeland to see a stranded whale, he sketched a walrus,[34] he gave five gold florins for some little long-tailed monkeys, and friends presented him with rarities from overseas whenever they could.

That for Dürer investigation of nature was never an end in itself, as it was for Leonardo, but always had to contribute to the greater glory of God, is proved by many works. In his water color of The Madonna with the Many Animals,[35] all the animals on this earth are given the task of making life pleasant and enchanting to the Infant Saviour in an earthly paradise. Fables and animal stories, like the one of the fox who lures the chickens by sweet music, are even inserted into the marginal illustrations of Emperor Maximilian's prayer book,[36] where the text deals with temptation. No wonder that it approaches medieval manuscripts like the Peterborough Psalter [37] in the Royal Library at Brussels, where a whole little zoo plays in the marginal ornaments.

To the immense experience of the outer world which arose in Dürer's art is added an experience of the inner world, the realm of the human soul. A wave of protest against the formalization and profanation of religion swept through the Western world about 1500. It was the ardent desire of the leading spirits to find an immediate way to God, to justify themselves through the strength of their belief instead through outer ecclesiastic formulas. A reforming spirit arose years before Luther's appearance; it had even more inner significance before the development of the new Protestant dogmatism. It is alive in Dürer's work beginning with the illustrations for the Apocalypse. Dürer experienced the sufferings of the Lord as a tragedy in his own life, as a frightful happening which occurs to the faithful mind everyday anew. This attitude is rooted in the religious subjectivism created by the German mystics in the fourteenth century.• With the artist, we attend the horrible moment when the body of the dead Lord falters in the arms of the man descending the ladder and almost seems to sink into our arms.[38] The artist in his inner soul so strongly shared the sufferings of the Lord that he identified himself with the "head covered with blood and wounds." One of his grandest late drawings is the Man of Sorrows (1522),[39] who bears Dürer's own features, full of the expression of a deep weariness (Fig. 10).

This religious attitude brought Dürer near to the rising tide of Protestantism. While his scholarly friends like Pirckheimer, Spengler, and Kratzer joined Luther for intellectual and political reasons, protesting against the corruption of Rome, Dürer followed him from a deep anxiety of his heart. Although he did not belong to the Protestant church community, he admired Luther because he showed the way through the turmoil of the time in a simple and powerful language. He sent his prints to him and ardently wished to portray him. In a letter to Spalatin, the chaplain of Frederick the Wise, he wrote in 1520: "God helping me, if ever I meet Dr. Martin Luther, I intend to draw his portrait carefully from life and to engrave it on copper, to be a lasting remembrance of a Christian man, who helped me out of great distress." Dürer made no difference between Luther and Erasmus of Rotterdam, whom he portrayed on his journey to the Netherlands,[40] unaware of the deep intellectual split between the two reformers, because to him the human and religious essence seemed to be the same in both. When Luther's simulated capture took place and the news reached Dürer in the Netherlands, he wrote a long prayer into his diary.

Oh God of heaven pity us! Oh Lord Jesus Christ pray for thy people! Deliver us at the fit time. . . . Oh all ye Christian men, help me deeply to bewail this man, inspired of God, and to pray Him yet to send us an enlightened man. Oh Erasmus of Rotterdam, where wilt thou stop? Behold how the wicked tyranny of worldly power, the might of darkness prevails. Hear, thou knight of Christ! Ride on by the side of the Lord Jesus. Guard the truth. Attain the martyr's crown.

When he wrote these words, Dürer in his thoughts identified Erasmus, the author of a Manual of the Christian Soldier,[41] with the hero of his famous engraving of 1513, Knight, Death, and Devil. The knight is the symbol of the Christian who calmly and fearlessly follows the way to the heavenly castle, unhampered, mocking Death and the Devil, who try in vain to lead him astray. He is followed by his faithful dog, symbol of divine zeal. To him, belief has become the sureness of inner experience, the confidence of a religious empiricism, which has discovered that not the acts of grace of an established church but the faith in the living word of Christ secures eternal gain. Thus, he means as much the beginning of a new time as does the discovery of the visible world.

II

Extremists in Art and Religion

In 1526 Albrecht Dürer completed the Four Apostles and dedicated them to the council of his native city Nuremberg as a spiritual heritage and admonition. The panels were provided with elaborate inscriptions chosen by the master himself from texts of those saintly men, which not only confirm Dürer's personal attitude in the religious struggle of his time — well known from his letters and diary — but also illuminate the spiritual situation in Germany after the establishment of Protestantism in a very revealing way. Therefore, I should like to quote them.

"All secular governors should take heed in these dangerous times that they may not accept human temptation instead of the Divine Word. God requests that nothing be added or taken away from his word. Therefore, listen to the warning of those excellent four men Peter, John, Paul, and Mark."

Peter in the second chapter of his second epistle writes as follows:

"But there were false prophets also among the people, even as there shall be false teachers among you, who privily shall bring in damnable heresies, even denying the Lord that bought them, and bring upon themselves swift destruction. And many shall follow their pernicious ways; by reason of whom the way of truth shall be evil spoken of. And through covetousness shall they with feigned words make merchandise of you: whose judgment now of a long time lingereth not, and their damnation slumbereth not."

John in the fourth chapter of his first epistle writes as follows:

"Beloved, believe not every spirit, but try the spirits whether they are of God: because many false prophets are gone out into the world. Hereby know ye the spirit of God: Every spirit that confesseth that Jesus Christ is come in the flesh is of God: And every spirit which confesseth not that Jesus Christ is come in the flesh is not of God: and this is that spirit of antichrist, whereof ye have heard that it should come; and even now already is it in the world."

St. Paul in his third chapter of his second epistle to Timothy writes as follows:

"This know also, that in the last days perilous times shall come. For men shall be lovers of their own selves, covetous, boasters, proud, blasphemers, disobedient to parents, unthankful, unholy, Without natural affection, trucebreakers, false accusers, incontinent, fierce, despisers of those that are good, Traitors, heady, highminded, lovers of pleasures more than lovers of God; having a form of godliness, but denying the power thereof: from such turn away. For this sort are they which creep into houses, and lead captive silly women laden with sins, led away with divers lusts, Ever learning and never able to come to the knowledge of the truth."

St. Mark writes in the twelfth chapter of his Gospel as follows: "And he said unto them in his doctrine, Beware of the scribes, which love to go in long clothing, and love salutations in the marketplaces. And the chief seats in the synagogues, and the uppermost rooms at feasts: Which devour widows' houses, and for a pretence make long prayers: these shall receive greater damnation."

With these passages, Dürer did not mean papal Rome and Catholicism, because the Lutheran Reformation had been firmly established in Nuremberg since 1525.[1] Yet the sudden cessation of the old ecclesiastic power released a multitude of emotional and revolutionary spiritual forces, which threatened to shatter not only orthodox Christianity but even the established foundations of society. Sectarians and prophets, illuminati and enthusiasts, apostles and preachers of the Baptists and Anabaptists, of the Bohemian and Moravian Brethren, roamed through the country. The peasant war raged in Southern Germany, in which religious emotion spurred the fight for a new economic and social order, intended to correspond to the spiritual communism of early Christianity. A potential of dynamic emotion, which is to be remarked in the Dürer of the Apocalypse as well as in the young Luther, now broke loose in a storm which threatened even the newly established creed of Protestantism. The chiliastic mood of 1500 resulted in violent manifestations. All established values were challenged. On the one hand, the prophecies of the enthusiasts flared up; on the other hand, a religious scepticism and nihilism came into being. These conflicts also threatened Nuremberg. There were not only the quarrels between the orthodox and the dissenting predicants, but even more radical disturbances. One of Dürer's own collaborators, the woodcutter Hieronymus Andreae, was imprisoned because of his connection with the revolutionary peasants. The painter Paulus Lautensack, a Sacramentarian, disquieted the city council with his apocalyptic ideas. Famous were the legal proceedings against three painter-engravers of Dürer's school: the brothers Barthel and Hans Sebald Beham and Georg Pencz. Barthel Beham, the creator of a most charming engraving full of worldly spirit, The Virgin at the Window (Bartsch, no. 8), uttered disbelief in Bible and Christ, baptism and communion. Pencz even confessed to being an atheist. They held all religious and secular authority in contempt. Thus, the fundamentals of the Lutheran creed were put in question. Lutheran orthodoxy now had to struggle just as much against heretic movements which had risen within its pale as in the Middle Ages the Catholic church had to struggle. We must understand the inscriptions of Dürer's Apostles as directed against those trends.[1]

In all times, established religion, anchored in the firm institutions of the church, has had to face the opposition of religious individualism and subjectivism. These forces are of greatest importance for its historical development, because they free the creative and imaginative energies which overcome torpid formalism and fill the religious life with new spiritual meaning. Many a saint was not far from being considered a heretic in his own times. From the late Middle Ages onward, the oppositional forces gained increasing importance in shaping the picture of religious life.

We have to distinguish between two main forms of these free religious forces: the mystics and the sects.[2] These forms are neither identical nor mutually exclusive; on the contrary, fusions of the two are very frequent. Yet in the same degree as there arose sects without the symptom of mystical illumination, there arose great mystics active within the framework of the church, although its stability was endangered through extreme forms of illumination. In the history of the Christian religion, both forms developed their creative power in the Middle Ages. In times of great revolutions of thought, like the beginning of the Renaissance, they may reach an extreme height. It is no wonder, then, that they find their reflection in the representational arts as well, either as a forecast or as an echo.

We shall deal with the form of mystical illumination and ecstatic inspiration first. The mystics of the twelfth century, Bernard of Clairvaux and Hugo of St. Victor, fitted themselves into the orthodox system of religious thought which rises like the petrified unison of the medieval cathedral. From the thirteenth century onward, religious subjectivism created increasingly individual and personal forms of thought which deviated from the orthodoxy formulated by the scholastics. The mendicant orders, especially the Franciscans, brought about a new ideal of brotherly community, poverty, and love of all things created by God, following the charitable community of Christ's disciples. The mystical spark contained in the teaching of St. Francis grew to a sacred glow in the works of the great German mystics and Dominicans of the fourteenth century, Master Ekkehard, the popular preacher Johannes Tauler, and the poet Heinrich Suso. The fourteenth century, distinguished by a highly expressive art, is the mystical century κατ᾽ ἐξοχήν. The rise of mysticism coincided with the increasing importance of the lay movement in religion, the culture of the cities, and the penetration of leading ideas into larger masses of people, although the essence of mysticism does not involve the forming of communities. It rather means either the fusing of the simple contemplative mind into the idea of God to a state of complete self-abandonment of the individual, or the visionary enhancement of the ecstatic soul. To the former type belong the aforementioned thinkers and preachers. Their teaching means the immediate approach to God in prayer and contemplation — union with God through the creative power of the soul itself, without the charismatic institutions of the church. To the latter type belong the visionaries and ecstatics who, in a state of rapture, described the glowing, unreal images rising before their eyes. The most important of these in the fourteenth century were St. Brigitta of Sweden and Santa Caterina da Siena.

The mystic knows only the spirit, its complete inner freedom and movement. The prophecy of the return of Christ and of the one thousand years' empire is to him the opening of his heart in love to Christ. Mysticism may remain in the precincts of the institutional church because its very essence soars above it. It cannot conflict with dogma, because it is undogmatic. The mystic presupposes the continuation of service in the traditional form because it does not interfere with his detached realm of spirit; he is an aristocrat of the mind, as humble as his standing may be. Mysticism stands beyond the creed, and the heritage of the Catholic mystics of the fourteenth century was taken up by the Lutheran Spiritualists of the sixteenth century. The Protestants were less tolerant of their mystics than the Catholics, and therefore forced them into radical opposition. Like the Catholic mystics, the Spiritualists demanded personal purification and sanctification of life, and did not acquiesce in the ablution of sin through the death of Christ. The ties between Catholic mysticism and Protestant spiritualism were strong in those tense days of the early sixteenth century. The gloom of chiliasm made their light shine all the brighter.

We comprehend that the works of the fourteenth-century mystics gained new importance in that era. Popular religious literature of the late fifteenth century shows the influence of Brigittine thought, and the most important work of the Saint, her *Revelations*, was published in Nuremberg in 1500 by Dürer's godfather Koberger in an edition illustrated by woodcuts which were made in Dürer's shop. A German edition which followed made possible a large distribution among contemporaries susceptible to these writings.

The language of St. Brigitta has a glowing, colorful intensity. The visions which she described while being in rapture have something of the visions of an artist. As a witness, she describes the Passion of Christ with an expressiveness and intuition which are worthy of a painter or sculptor. She conjures up the sufferings of Christ and the Glory of the Virgin in images of an incredible boldness and ecstatic clarity, images which she thought she actually saw in reality. That her visions were apt to inspire the imagination of a great painter is obvious. They did so in reality. The greatest work of religious painting in Germany, the high altar of the church of Isenheim, a monastery of the knightly order of the hospitalers of St. Anthony near Colmar in Alsace, was deeply inspired by St. Brigitta's visions.

The master who created this immortal work has come down to us in historiography under the name of Matthias Grünewald.[3] Documents found in the last decades have made evident that his true name was Mathis Gothart-Neithart.[4] We know less of his life than of any of his famous contemporaries in Germany. His biography is clear only in parts; much of it, the year of his birth, for instance, still lies in darkness. He was court painter to the archbishop electors of Mainz, the cardinals Uriel von Gemmingen and Albrecht von Brandenburg, and died in 1528. The country of the Main and Middle Rhine was the area of his activity. He seems to have been born in Würzburg, and to have belonged to the same stock as Dürer, the Franconian. For many years he was settled in the town of Seligenstadt. Aschaffenburg, Mainz, Frankfurt, and Halle were the changing places of his activity, yet his greatest work he did for Isenheim.

The Isenheim Altar is dated 1515. The master worked on it probably from 1513 to 1515, as contracts for the shrine drawn up in these years are known. Preceptors of the order, whose main task was the hospitalization and cure of sick people, were the Italians Johan de Orliac and Guido Guersi who, strangely enough, entrusted the greatest Northern painter of their time with the noble task. The altar consisted of a shrine of sculptures by the carver Niclas Hagnower and three pairs of wings, two movable ones and one fixed.[5] The carved predella, too, could be closed by a pair of wings. All those wings, consisting of wooden panels, were painted by Grünewald. The biblical subjects range from the Annunciation to the Resurrection; the legendary subjects narrate the story of the patron saint to whom church and altar were dedicated, St. Anthony. The unusual selection and interpretation of the subjects gave rise to much speculation about the true meaning of the paintings and their combination. The extravagant imagination of a highly personal artistic mind seemed to have been responsible not only for the strangely expressive forms but also for the surprising iconographical program.

The altar is a so-called transforming altar which offers different aspects on high holidays, Sundays, and weekdays. On weekdays, the somber and mournful Crucifixion (Fig. 11) looked from the closed shrine into the nave, a work of such tremendous and dismal grandeur of expression that nothing on earth seems to equal it. The Crucified rises in the center, nailed down on a coarse cross of raw timber. He is of supernatural dimensions. His size is almost twice that of the other humans, and stands in no rational relation to them, as in medieval art the spiritually important surpasses the ranks of minor beings. The explanation is given by St. John the

Baptist, standing on the right, who points to the Crucified and speaks the words: "He must grow, I must shrink." The dead body, showing all signs of horrible torture, indeed seems to grow, even to break up the framework of the altar. His legs are twisted and cramped, his fingers point in shrill pain to heaven, his head sinks down, and his mouth seems to be paralyzed in the last agony. Hundreds of wounds cover the strong, wrenched body. It grows out of the blackish blue night of the sky and the ghostly green half-light of the landscape as if it were a condensation of the tense mood of the end of the world which holds nature in chains. The color of the body is based on that olive or greenish hue which is found in Sienese paintings of the Trecento. Here, it becomes the color of decay, shown without mercy and mitigation to the pious onlooker that he may be shattered to the depths of his soul. St. Anselmus describes how the body of the Lord, lovely before, was torn after the flagellation as by leprosy. The blood extravasates in cascades of mystically glowing red. All this was represented by Grünewald with breathtaking immediacy.

Where else do we have descriptions of the catastrophe on Golgotha of a similar ghastly realism and mystical elevation? In the thought and art of the fourteenth century. About twenty years ago, a Catholic scholar, Rector Heinrich Feurstein, made the important discovery that the writings of St. Brigitta were a source of inspiration to the ingenious painter.[6] In them we find a related extremism of the excited religious fantasy. It was the trend of the growing religious subjectivism in the late Middle Ages to live up to the sufferings of Christ as a personal experience. This St. Brigitta did in her visions, which she described in the *Revelations on the Life and Passion of Jesus Christ and His Mother the Holy Virgin Mary*.

The crown of thorns was impressed on his head; it covered half of the forehead. The blood ran in many rills. . . . Then the color of death spread. . . . After He had expired, the mouth gaped, so that the spectators could see the tongue, the teeth, and the blood in the mouth [Fig. 13]. The eyes were cast down. The knees were bent to one side; the feet were twisted around the nails as if they were on hinges. . . . The cramped fingers and arms were stretched.

How much of Grünewald's images seems to have been foreshadowed in these writings! Nowhere in art do hands speak such an eloquent language as in the Crucifixion. How the numb fingers of Christ radiate pain and woe! How full of meaning is the emphatically stretched pointing finger of the Evangelist's hand! The immensity of inner tension almost threatens to disrupt the painting. A similar tension is revealed in some fourteenth-century sculptures, the so-called "mystics' crosses," which are indeed contemporary with St. Brigitta's writings or even somewhat earlier, like the Crucified in St. Maria im Kapitol, Cologne (Fig. 14), which dates from the early fourteenth century. What flaring color expresses in Grünewald's panel is here expressed by line and form, saturated with the mysticism of suffering. If the term "expressionism" is justified in the fine arts, so it is with these sculptures and the paintings of Grünewald. To the degree that St. Brigitta's writings inspired Grünewald, she herself seems to have been inspired by sculptures of this kind. A profile view of this cross reveals the blending of highest abstraction and crude realism as shown in the ribs and the swollen veins of the legs. St. Brigitta describes it: "The ribs protruded and could be counted. After the moisture was consumed, the stomach receded to the back." We know a lost Crucifixion by Grünewald through a seventeenth-century copy, which belonged probably to an altar of St. Magdalen in Isenheim.[7] It represents a dialogue of the lonely Saint with the Crucified, full of unfathomable woe.[8] The historical event becomes here in the mystical conception the complaint of tortured humanity. We see the emaciated body of Christ in the jagged silhouette of a casual profile aspect, which reveals its nearness to the fourteenth-century sculpture, and it is reasonable to assume that Grünewald received stimulation not only from mystic writings but also from mystic works of art. Never would excessive emotion have induced Dürer to give up tectonic balance in such a high degree as Grünewald did here. Grünewald's *œuvre* is small compared to that of other Old German masters; besides the Isenheim altar, it consists of a few panels and drawings. The representation of the Crucified occupies an unusually large part of his work; it occurs in ever new variations, and a Crucifixion was also the last work which the master left incomplete when he died. A large drawing (Karlsruhe, Museum) blends the twisted body of Christ with the twists of rough timber, of uneven knotted bark and spiny thorns. The touch of Grünewald's chalk drawings is, with all its comprehensive vigor, extremely delicate.[9] The vision of the great painter is manifest in the rendering of rough and smooth surfaces with the most intensive feeling for materials. Grünewald follows nature to the smallest detail without losing the great context. Beside the giant Christ on the Isenheim Altar kneels the small figure of the Magdalen, giving herself up to lamentation which flows out of her in a wave of sorrow. The gesture, the wringing of her hands, discloses all her agony of soul. These hands are perhaps the most important part of the figure. No less expressive are those in the figure of the fainting Mary, who, enveloped in a white shroud, sinks back into the arms of St. John, almost more dead than the Crucified in his ghostly aliveness. St. Brigitta writes: "The violence of the dolor contracted her heart so much, that every limb of her most sacred body was found wanting." For her hands, Grünewald prepared in a magnificent half-length female study in which we can admire, almost as if seen through a magnifying glass, a sensitive richness of pictorial detail which we never meet in Dürer's more synthesized drawings.[10]

On Sundays, the mournful seriousness of the Golgotha scene disappeared with the opening of the outer pair of wings of the Isenheim Altar, and the ecstatic jubilation of the Angels' Concert flowed in great waves into the church (Fig. 12). The picture surface is divided into two halves with regard to iconography, composition, and color. The left half of the central part is filled with a chapel in wildly flamboyant Late Gothic. Its sweeps, arches, crockets, and finials seem to turn into living, climbing, creeping plants, among which prophets of the Old Testament dwell, excitedly gesticulating. The masonry shines forth in a radiant polychromy of cinnabar, violet, yellow, and blue. Inside the chapel, the Holy Virgin kneels in glorified, transfigured state. She glows like a celestial vision, one color flowing over into the other. The deep moss-green in the seam of her mantle goes over into deep greenish blue, changes into a purple glow from within, burns in a fiery red, and sublimates in the yellow glare of the head. Such insufficient indications of the magic of the coloring can be only a slight hint of the expression of the ecstatic and visionary which there prevails. Out of the impenetrable night which fills the arches of the chapel emerge hosts of adoring angels and supernatural beings in a bluish spectral light, strangely shaped, framed by emanations of light as by peacock wings. Their jubilation turns into musical sound with three large angels, who, enraptured, play on viole da gamba and braccia, one of them being a seraph in a green coat of feathers. The spectral light in the left panel gives way to the radiant day in the right panel, where Mary as Holy Mother enjoys the Babe in tender happiness, amid the implements of the nursery which are scattered around forming a still-life in the open air. Nevertheless, she receives queenly distinction through the carmine of her garment which purls and floats in the light like water or smoke. A radiant scene with towering high mountains expands behind her in shining blue, violet, and iridescent green. An ultramarine cloud settles down, overflooded by yellowish light which streams from the vision of God the Father, sending down myriads of angels.

For the ecstatic jubilation of this painting we also find parallels in St. Brigitta's writings: in the Angelic Sermon on the Excellency of the Holy Virgin Mary, which was a prescribed reading of her order during the days of the week. Mary in the Chapel is the idea of the Mother of God. "In this perfection, thou wast from eternity before the eye of God, and has received thy blessed body from clear and pure elements." "The blessed body of the child Mary was comparable to a pure vase of crystal." Grünewald illustrates this by placing a beautiful decanter of Venetian glass before the Virgin. "The angels burned from love since the first moment of thy creation and jubilated." "As much as the Holy Virgin was full of joy more than all other mothers when she contemplated her Babe, she was full of sorrow in prescience of His sufferings." "The angels floated up and down between heaven and earth like motes in a sunbeam." Several years later, Grünewald painted another image of the maternal happiness of Mary, now in the church of Stuppach (Fig. 16), full of gayest splendor, of magic brilliancy of color and light — a painting in which the celestial and earthly paradise blend into unison. A mighty cathedral rises behind the Virgin. It illustrates the revelation of God to the Virgin on the condition of His church under the symbol of a decaying cathedral. "I am the Virgin whom the Son of God has dignified. . . . Therefore, I abide in continuous prayer above the world like a rainbow above the clouds." Mary's halo turns in the picture into a flaming rainbow. To St. Brigitta, the Virgin spoke: "I was in verity a beehive, when the most sacred bee, the Son of God, took abode in my womb." So we see beehives in the enchanting flower garden, full of the fragrant spell of summer.

On the left of the so-called "Sunday side" of the Isenheim altar, the Glorification of Mary is flanked by the Annunciation, where Mary's fright at the appearance of the Angel is depicted with the intensity of an almost physical shock. The right wing contains the Resurrection of Christ. The Spiritualists taught that Christ's body since the beginning of the creation had been supernatural and spiritual flesh. As in Grünewald's panel Christ flares up in the starry Easter night as a phantom of light, as the whitish-blue of the shroud and the burning carmine-red of the clothes leap like flames consumed by the yellowish incandescence of the face, we see how painting was able to achieve and express a similar spiritualization and transubstantiation of matter. The painting turns into liquid fire. The pigments are translucent like glass.

Grünewald knew how to render this highest immateriality of light together with the most exquisite substantiality of materials in his drawings, in which he used only the monochrome of black chalk combined with white heightenings on the yellowish paper ground. St. Dorothy (Berlin, Kupferstichkabinett) seems to be a condensation of light, standing almost without weight, her garment flowing as if it were suspended in the open air (Fig. 15). This garment, with the rich design of its pleating, is a miracle of precious rendering of silky, reflecting, rustling stuffs. The curving and swinging of the figure of the Saint, who seems to balance like the Infant Saviour on the sphere beside her, have nothing in common with the firm stability of Dürer's figures. They are reminiscent of the highly expressive figures of the early fifteenth-century paintings in Grünewald's native region. An altarpiece from his home town of Seligenstadt (now in Darmstadt, Hessisches Landesmuseum) shows four female Saints in the so-called "soft style," the German version of the "international style." They are the ancestors of Grünewald's female figures. His ties with late medieval art are so strong that critics like to consider him as the last representative of the Middle Ages, and to contrast him with Dürer as the first Renaissance master. This interpretation is not quite correct. The medieval element in Grünewald's art is not the result of an uninterrupted stream of medieval art, but is a conscious harking back to a great idealistic art of former centuries. His approach may be compared with Michelangelo's going back to Masaccio and Giotto, with Dürer's medieval revival in the Apocalypse. This is something different from the immediate continuance of the Late Gothic as we see it in Dürer's beginnings. It is the indication of a new spirit, striving for the great and lofty, which is one of the essentials of the new era no less than its eager search for realities, its empiricism. Thus Grünewald is in line with the great progressive history-making masters of his time.

The *intentional revival* of features of medieval art, past for one or more centuries, is a symptom which we notice in both masters, Dürer and Grünewald alike, and in both it signifies a modern, advancing trend. It materializes in the two masters differently. Dürer's great static nature, thinking in tectonic terms, found its counterpart in the heroic centuries of early and high medieval art from 1000 to 1300. The violently emotional and dynamic spirit of Grünewald found his rather in the mystic era of the fourteenth century and the beginning of the fifteenth century.

The convulsions of Grünewald's great emotional art, too, are documentations of the spirit of the new time. They belong in the realm of psychical experience. Grünewald's highly personal concepts, although he was court painter of an archbishop, may often have gone to the limit of that which is tolerable for the church. The biography of the master, written by the seventeenth-century painter Sandrart,[11] mentions that he painted in 1511 a Transfiguration of Christ for the Church of the Predicant Friars in Frankfort. In the same church was Dürer's altar of the Assumption of the Virgin painted for Jacob Heller, which Grünewald provided with two fixed wings representing the Saints Lawrence and Cyriacus. The two artists were in occasional contact — Dürer once donated some of his printed art to Grünewald. Grünewald's Transfiguration has been lost, yet drawings for some figures of Apostles are preserved (Dresden, Kupferstichkabinett). One of them shows Saint Peter prostrated on the ground (Fig. 17). The storm of holy light which roars over him is not greater than the storm of emotion which shakes his soul. We face an excess of religious fervor, as it grasped the minds of the ecstatics and enthusiasts, as it roared through the movement of the Spiritualists. A head of a screaming angel (Fig. 18) reveals in its stirring, frightening pose a similar exaltation.

There must have been links between Grünewald and the religious extremists of his time. When the peasant war swept through the country, many of the cities in which the artisans had gained the upper hand joined the revolutionaries, among them the artist's home town Seligenstadt. In 1526 he was dismissed as court painter, and we find him again as a hydraulic engineer in the service of the Protestant community of Halle, which was strongly opposed to the archbishop; there he died in 1528. In the inventory of his estate is mentioned a so-called "roll of sedition," a testimony and warrant given by a reliable person in favor of a fellow citizen who had been guilty of sympathizing with the rebels. Furthermore, there was found a nailed-up drawer which was filled with Lutheran books ("Lutherische Scharteken"). There might have been writings of the Spiritualists and heretics among them, that the master hid them so carefully. A strange drawing (Fig. 19) is still a puzzle to the scholars: three ugly heads of men grown together, surrounded by the fire of a flashing halo. It was considered as a mockery of the Trinity. The representation is too serious for a mockery, although it must have been anathema to an orthodox Catholic mind. The heads in all their ugliness are filled with holy expression, like the apostles of the rebellious artisans and peasants, of the people of the low classes, over whom "the spirit came" and made them rise. The representation of the Trinity in the form of three male persons was frequently considered as heretic in the sixteenth century.[12] Spiritualism opposed the dogma of Christ as the God Man, because it knew Christ only in the spirit. Hence, it opposed also the dogma of the Trinity, which it regarded as emanation of *one* being, just as we see it in Grünewald's drawing.

Grünewald's influence was strong, mainly in the region of the Main, and the Middle and Upper Rhine, although he did not form a proper school as Dürer did. Traces of his strange emotionalism can be found in the art of Hans Baldung, who lived and worked

in Strassburg. He came from Dürer's studio, yet later he approached the great pictorial and rhapsodic touch of Grünewald.
Many of his works have a worldly, almost pagan flavor, yet some
of his religious representations vibrate from an inner tension which
is congenial to Grünewald's expressionism; for instance the woodcut of the Lamentation for Christ (Bartsch, no. 5), which represents a violent outburst of grief over the strangely foreshortened
body of Christ. In another woodcut (Bartsch, no. 43), little angels painfully drag the corpse, feet foremost, in a pose very ir-
reverent from the standpoint of religious convention, to heaven,
where the Father, the Holy Ghost, and innumerable little angels,
emanating from a ray of celestial light, are ready to receive him.
Never before had the return of the Son to the Father been represented in such a dramatic and unceremonious way, contradicting
every dogmatic notion.

The art of Baldung leads on to Switzerland. A similar freeing
from every dogmatism, whether Catholic or Protestant, is to be
noticed in the work of the Swiss reformers, Zwingli and the
Baptists. Dürer felt attracted by the clear and realistic approach
of Zwingli, although Luther condemned him and the Baptists as
violently as the Spiritualist apostates in his own church. The Swiss
mind, in its religious notions, is strongly rooted in this world,
where it has to prove itself actively. The Passion of Christ in excessive realism shows the hardships and tortures which a brave
fighter for the cause of God has to pass through. While Grünewald in the Isenheim Altar lets his St. Anthony be tortured by
monsters of a feverish imagination, the draughtsman and goldsmith Urs Graf of Basel in a drawing of 1520 [13] applies the same
physical violence to the Scourging of Christ, which degenerates
into a wild lansquenets' riot. The poor victim is beaten and tram-
pled to death in an infernal whirl of movement, the brutality of
which reflects some of the time's bitter realities. Contemporary
documents recount that in some countries sectarians, mainly Baptists, were exposed to similar treatment.

At this point we must say a few words about the second form
of free religious forces, the sects. The established church tends to
make the state and the ruling classes subservient to its purposes.
The sects rise from the lower classes, which oppose state and so-

ciety. They attempt to resuscitate the spirit of the Sermon on the Mount, of early Christianity in a small community united by the bonds of altruism and brotherly love. The Baptists, whose movement started from radicals in Zurich, in 1525, represent the pure type of a sect. Baptism of adults, priesthood of lay people, refusal of war and oath, and community of goods are characteristic of the Baptist movement. Its adherers were persecuted with fire and sword by both churches, the Catholic and the Protestant, because they saw in them a threat to society. There is much of the spirituality of the young Luther in the Baptist movement. As Luther saw in the dissolution of the existing church an indication of the imminent end of all things, so a chiliastic and eschatologic feeling reigned among the Baptists. The desertion of the masses predicted in the Apocalypse has arrived. The fate of Christianity rests with few. Luther in his beginnings was considered as a flaming spirit, a prophet and overturner, as a woodcut by Hans Baldung [14] portrays him. This spirit continued in the mystics among Luther's own followers who deserted him in later years when he turned dogmatist – Hans Denck and Andreas Karlstadt, who both were in contact with Dürer, Thomas Münzer and Caspar Schwenkfeld. These Spiritualists tended not so much toward the forming of sects as they did toward complete freedom of spirit. Institutions and sacraments lose importance. The inner light which illuminates the soul is the true revelation of Christ.[15]

In those critical days, in that enthusiastic mood of the end of the world and beginning of a new reign, the sects and the Protestant mystics approached each other. They had to battle the same opposition. The originally peaceful Baptist movement, where it met with radical combatant trends deriving from the Hussites and Taborites, turned into the gospel of violence. This was the case with the peasant movement and with the Anabaptists of Westphalia. The idea of the evangelical reign of Christ on earth joined with radical political rebellion against the ruling powers. Mass excitement, as in all revolutions, was foreboded by religious hysteria. One of its phenomena was the cult of the Beautiful Mary in Regensburg, brought to life by the Dominican Dr. Balthasar Huebmaier who finally ended as a Baptist at the stake in Vienna. The miraculous image of the cult, painted by Albrecht Altdorfer, represents the Virgin, pale like a somnambulist, standing against a background which palpitates like an aurora borealis in gold and blood red.[16] Dürer inscribed a woodcut, representing the veneration of this image, with the following words: "This specter rose in Regensburg against the Holy Writ. . . . God help us that we may not dishonor His holy mother, Amen."[17]

As Huebmaier joined the Baptists from the Catholic camp, so Thomas Münzer joined the rebellious peasants from the Lutheran.[18] Münzer's teaching was a fusion of mystical ideas with the revolution of the Bohemian brethren with whom he was connected for some time. He considered it permitted to bring about Christian unity by violence, if the ruling powers failed. So the vortex of the peasant war finally engulfed him. After its bloody suppression, Münzer was beheaded with other leaders.

Münzer had his counterpart in the fine arts in the painter Joerg Ratgeb.[19] He belonged to the school of Suabia, and was in the service of the Duke of Württemberg at Stuttgart in 1508. He was a painter in the forefront of his era. Like Grünewald, Dürer, and Altdorfer, he certainly had been in the Netherlands, and perhaps also in Venice. Ratgeb's ties to the lower classes, the simple people, were strong — his wife had been a serf. In all his high pictorial culture, he had a strong inclination for the Biblical primitivism of the poor peasants and artisans. The "poor in spirit" were to him the heirs of the kingdom of heaven. This is more than an artistic, this is a human, attitude; yet it is reflected also in his paintings. Most expressive are the huge panels of the Herrenberger Altar (1518–19) with the story of Christ and the apostles.

Sometimes it happens that an artist predestined for the most exquisite handling of color and design purposely gives up all refinement and strives for a harsh, primitive, and rustic style. Intentional impoverishment can grant the gain of new values of expression. We find this phenomenon not only in modern art but also in that of earlier centuries. Ratgeb is an example. This artist, whose exquisite color taste and feeling for decorative pattern could have made him one of the best representatives of a highly cultivated art of painting in Germany, gave up all these qualities to become a prophet of the "poor in spirit." The Resurrection of the Herrenberger Altar (Fig. 20) is a huge peasant painting.

Christ, stiff as a wood carving, rises from his tomb. The guards are rough country fellows whose awkward silhouettes form a curious pattern with the many objects scattered on the ground. The panel offers the aspect of a primitive broad sheet. The colors, either variegated or faded to pale, chalky hues, are discordant in tone. Rays of a spectral bluish light cross the air. Christ is indeed a spirit. He has penetrated the tomb without effort, because he is less substantial than his drapery. His translucid body is uplifted in a miraculous act of levitation. Ratgeb must have known Grünewald's works. He achieved a similar spiritualization, while neglecting all that pictorial culture and refinement which was so essential for Grünewald.

The Farewell of the Apostles takes place in a dreary autumnal landscape. Bare trees, birds, rocks, and buildings fill the picture surface with an exotic pattern. How exquisitely path and wall sweep up to the towering castle! The apostles are awkward artisans and peasants like their master. They try to hide their emotion in a touching way. In all their humbleness and queerness, they are filled with a fanatic piety. Theirs was the type of the lay preachers whom the peasants of the Bundschuh and the rebellious artisans of the old cities followed.

As in our time, then, too, artistic and political radicalism sometimes went hand in hand; and this was the case with Ratgeb. He was delegated by the revolutionary city to serve as councilor to the belligerent peasants. When the peasant war was suppressed with greatest cruelty, Ratgeb was captured as one of the spiritual leaders and quartered.

It is a dark chapter of past history which the fate of these Spiritualists illustrates. Irrationality and cruelty, deeply rooted in the German mind, played an important part in it. But the altars erected in the German churches during this period teach us that amidst all this gloom and anxiety works of an eternal beauty arose.

III

The New Attitude toward Nature

The Discoverers of Landscape in Painting and Science

O N OPENING the shrine of the Isenheim Altar, we see on the left wing the scene of the visit of St. Anthony to St. Paul, the hermit in the wilderness depicted by Grünewald. Here the art of the master reaches its climax. Evening spreads over the valley, in which trees of the German forest are interspersed with exotic palms. It is an aboriginal, a magic landscape, which looks as if the waters of the deluge had just receded. Rocks darken in deep, velvety brown; stems rise, gray like the bodies of scaly animals; black mosses drip from the branches. Deer cross the wilderness with soundless step, merging with the dusk. Misty hues float through a mysterious glen in the background, where beyond a dark river the silent majesty of the blue, high forest rises. It is overtowered by mountain peaks whose aerial shapes catch the last evening light and softly glow in a most tender rose. The whole color symphony is unified as in a painting by Titian.

This extraordinary feeling of nature does not appear for the first time in German painting with Grünewald. In a painting (Fig. 21) done some years earlier, in 1511 (actually a sheet of vellum mounted on wood), there is represented the meeting of St. George with the dragon. It is difficult to distinguish the figure of the Saint in his plumed helmet from the thicket of the high forest. The overwhelming richness of uncouth nature fills the little panel. Tall beeches form a tight network with the undergrowth; one form is interlaced with the other. The forest as a unit is supposed to enter the picture space. Although we see only a part of it, its unlimited extension in height and depth is suggested. A soft breeze seems to move the branches, so that the high lights of the leaves glitter. The forest is the main content of the picture, while the holy legend is reduced to a sparkling color spot. The painter of this astounding little picture is Albrecht Altdorfer, the most important representative of a school which originated in the Danube valley and is therefore called the Danube School. With this school, a new feeling of nature arose, which seemingly influenced Grünewald when he painted the two hermits. Nor were the artists of the Danube School the very beginners of the new mode. They stood on the shoulders of the young Dürer, who showed the way in his amazing water colors. There, for the first time, we find the complete absorption in the miracle of nature. Dürer focused his interest on a motif which fascinated him, which he selected from its surroundings, and which he carefully portrayed. Compare for instance the study of a fir tree in the British Museum (Lippmann, no. 221). We can hardly speak of one significant motif in Altdorfer's painting. It contains many motifs, but it is indifferent to their isolated beauty. What fascinated the painter, what he thought should be mirrored in the small panel, was the total impression, the exuberance and growth of nature itself. This feeling of nature goes beyond Dürer, who did not especially cultivate landscape as subject matter in his later years. This feeling for visual totality, not halting at an isolated faithful study but carrying the whole concept of a picture, made possible landscape painting as an art in its own right. This important category of modern art begins in Northern Europe with the Renaissance. It could not have originated if the predisposition for it had not existed in the general intellectual situation. We now have to consider this state of affairs briefly.

During the Middle Ages, the study of nature had formed a part of the great speculative world system on the theological basis. With the rise of empiricism, in which the fine arts played an important role, investigation became increasingly independent of its theological limitations. Theology continued, as materialistic scepticism had not yet destroyed the belief in the divine revelation, while the study of nature became closely linked up with philosophy. Both trends, the theological and the scientific, centered in the idea of the Divine Creator. As the scientific thought endeavored to understand the universe as an embodiment of God, who pervades it to its smallest atom, the historians commonly speak of the *pantheism* in philosophy and science of the Renaissance. This pantheism found expression in the representational arts also, and we shall deal with this problem below.

First we must consider briefly the role of the empirical sciences in this whole development. The origins of modern biology, physiology, and chemistry were closely linked up with medical science at the beginning of this era.[1] Rational science in the modern sense was as yet unknown, especially in Northern Europe. Magic, mystical, superstitious notions, partly of medieval, partly of ancient, origin, were frequently intertwined with the scientific discoveries. Mathematics and physics with their doctrine of quantities and method of analysis were not as dominating as in the seventeenth century. Numbers were believed to have magic properties. Intuitive perception of the total and empirical investigation of the detail were more in use than abstract calculation starting from axioms. We have already noted Dürer's keen interest in nature, in rare animals and plants. Zoological gardens were established in the European cities with overseas connections. The universities of Padua and Pisa introduced botanical gardens. Germany and the Netherlands, where botanists like Brunfels and Fuchs, L'Écluse and L'Obel were active, followed. Herbals with woodcut illustrations were common in Germany during the fifteenth century.[2] The metallurgist Agricola gained geological experiences in the mines of Bohemia. The searching intellect did not halt at empirical experiences. Philosophy attempted to draw a synthesis. The French philosopher Carolus Bovillus (Charles de Bouelles), a contemporary of Dürer who wrote a book on the senses, compared the macrocosm to an animated being with its rhythm of life, alternately awake and sleeping.[3] Light, clouds, and atmosphere in their influence on the visibility of the celestial bodies were observed by him as much as by the painters.

Philosophy tried to discover the deeper reasons, the moving forces behind all occurrences in nature. Medicine did the same, in order to master those secret forces and to subdue them to its purposes. The approach to nature of the great physicians Paracelsus and Cardanus was as much synthesizing and intuitive with regard to the total as it was experimental and empirical in details. Medicine had to deal with many fields in this early stage, so the way to philosophical synthesis offered itself. Paracelsus, the most famous physician of the time, one of its great representative spirits, made it his task to understand the secret forces in nature, the organic growth and decay of all things. Thus, as a scientist, he followed the same aims as the discoverers of landscape in painting. They started their work one decade earlier than Paracelsus, however, and we shall therefore deal with them first. It is surprising how often the formulations of Paracelsus seem to be literary interpretations of the painters' new and pioneering way of visualizing nature.

The birthplace of the new landscape art was one of the loveliest countries on earth, Austria. Whoever has experienced the spell of its charming scenery of high mountains, hills, lakes, and rivers will understand that it was bound to prompt this new art as soon as the eyes of the artists were ready to perceive scenic beauties. We have seen how Dürer's eyes were opened when he crossed to Italy through the valleys of the Tyrol. The problems of landscape painting were taken up especially by the schools working in the Danube valley between Passau and Vienna.[4] It is significant that their painters favored saintly legends interwoven with the life of nature as subjects. One of them was the story of the holy Margrave Leopold, Austria's patron saint. According to the legend, a storm robbed the Margravine of her veil, a cherished memento of her mother. The Margrave, hunting one day in the forest, was led by the Holy Virgin to an elderbush, which had caught the veil. In gratitude, he erected the monastery Klosterneuburg on the sacred spot. The painter Rueland Frueauf the Younger, in 1501, recounted this story in a cycle of small altar panels.[5] In it the hunting party leaves the castle and enters the forests of the Danube (Fig. 22). A fraction of the scene is shown, suggested by the slender shape of the panel, as if the observer were catching an accidental glimpse. The modeling is careful and the colors shine like jewels. Rocks, trees, and fields are designed in the most subtle and fanciful linework, stylized, yet saturated with the flavor of nature. The Margrave rides to the hunt in full state like the king in the fairy tale. We notice two significant features in these paintings: first, the magic fairy-tale character which clings to most of the landscape representations of the German Renaissance, and second, the poetical spell, the enhancement, the dreamlike quality, which is very different from the scientific Dutch landscape of the seventeenth century. One can see the softly rolling fields of the picture of the boar hunt today from the windows of the monastery, and yet it is landscape as if seen in a dream, landscape as expression, not as optical statement.

Under the rulership of Emperor Maximilian I, the Germans did not behave as ruthless overlords in the lovely country as in these recent years of terror, but a good-neighbor policy existed between Austria and Germany. They exchanged the best talents in the artistic and intellectual fields. Artists and scholars from Franconia, Bavaria, Suabia, and Switzerland came at the beginning of the century to Austria, not only to find work there but also inspiration. The humanists Conrad Celtes and Johannes Cuspinian taught as professors at the University of Vienna, where Zwingli was enrolled as a student. The painters were certainly not least attracted by the beauty of the scenery. From Suabia came Joerg Breu the Elder, from Franconia Lucas Cranach, from Bavaria the brothers Albrecht and Erhard Altdorfer. They obtained commissions from the churches, monasteries, and burghers in the cities. They let the spell of the Austrian scenery enter into their paintings. They received inspiration from the native painters and returned it to them richly. Thus, the Danube School originated.

In 1500, Joerg Breu from Augsburg painted a folding altar for the Cistercian monastery Zwettl which I discovered some years ago — now it is considered to be a landmark of Old German painting.[6] It recounts the legend of St. Bernard, the founder of the order. In the figure composition, it depends upon the masters of Augsburg; in the surprisingly modern landscapes, it follows Frueauf. Here we see St. Bernard with his fellow monks at the harvest. The simple charm of the landscape of Lower Austria is rendered in the most perfect manner. The waves of the golden grain move softly in the breeze. The hills roll up and down, followed by the country road which is lined with single trees and wayside crosses. One feels invited to stroll along through the peaceful country, from one old town, castle, or monastery to the next.

About the same time, Lucas Cranach, the later court painter

of the Electors of Saxony and portraitist of the reformers, discovered landscape in Austria.⁷ We know from his own testimony that he stayed at the beginning of the century in Vienna. In 1502, he painted a penitent St. Jerome in the wilderness (Fig. 23; Vienna, Kunsthistorisches Museum). The Saint is a forest dweller, a little wild man of Herculean shape. The vigorous figure shows that the painter was familiar with Dürer's style. It was the great merit of Cranach and Breu to have brought to Austria information about the powerful art of the young Dürer, whose prints began to spread his fame. St. Jerome kneels in a clearing in the forest; his red cardinal's cloak and his lion blend with the honey-colored rocks. Ragged pine and fir trees grow high; their dark olive-green branches, designed in little flames, are covered with sparkling high lights. Birches are hung with the silvery gray of dripping mosses. Birds dwell in the branches, among them an owl and a parrot which have sidereal connotations. The whole picture seems to hum with summer. Between the dark trees, one can see the light splendor of the country at the foot of the Alps, the peaks of which appear on the horizon in icy blue.

Painting realizes here for the first time in history what philosophy established in the notion of the *microcosm*. The philosopher and scientist meant by the word "microcosm" first of all man, who was supposed to mirror on a small scale everything that the macrocosm, the universe, contains. This involves the fact that the macrocosm, too, was considered as an organism. The smallest thing was inseparably connected with the total, as in landscape art the foreground is with the background by means of organic structure and atmosphere. Thus, pantheism considered God as dwelling in the infinite of the universe and in the smallest part of it at the same time. *The microcosm mirrors the macrocosm.*⁸ This relation became reality in the works of the early landscape painters.

The paintings which Cranach did in Austria are his best, full of tremendous vitality and glowing vigor of color. If he had stayed for good in the inspiring country, perhaps he would have become as great a painter as Grünewald. His later paintings never reached this high level, with exception of the portraits, in which he knew how to keep his old vigor.

At this point, Albrecht Altdorfer joined Cranach.⁹ He was a

Bavarian and a native of Regensburg. In the sixteenth century, Bavarians were more closely related to their Austrian neighbors in the Danube valley than to any other stock. The great river connected a similar landscape, people, and art — people of a gay, positive temper, enjoying the beauty of their earthly paradise. It was a matter of course that Altdorfer in his very beginnings should turn up in Austria, doing some woodcuts for the monastery of Mondsee.[10] He became acquainted with the Austrian works of Cranach; a little panel representing St. Jerome, dated 1507 (Berlin, Deutsches Museum), is clearly influenced by Cranach's picture of the Church Father. It is softer, more lyrical in mood than Cranach's dynamic painting, yet the blending of the figure with its surrounding goes even beyond Cranach. In Cranach's panel, all objects preserve a vigorous plasticity. In Altdorfer's painting, the objects seem to be colored condensations of atmosphere. Although the organization of Altdorfer's work is much less clear than Cranach's, it surpasses the latter in pictorial unification. Altdorfer's handling of the brush like a drawing pen also contributes to this unification. A design of sweeping lines and pretty curls goes through both the landscape and the figure, increasing their unity. The figure seems to grow out of the earth like trees and plants. This is no mere metaphor. Paracelsus spoke of it clearly in his *Third Book of Philosophy*, when he compared plants with the human organism: "This growth . . . is similar to man; it has the bark as its skin, the root as its head and hair; it has its body and senses; its sensibility in the stem, that it dies, if you hurt it; it is adorned by flowers and fruits as man by the ability of hearing, seeing and speaking." "The body is a wood, and life a fire which consumes it." Some of Altdorfer's creatures, indeed, look like mandrakes. In 1506, he represented a Witches' Sabbath in a clair-obscure drawing, executed with white and dark ink on brown prepared paper.[11] The fabulous creatures seem to grow out of the curls of the foliage, the sweep of the branches. Such beings were then considered as realities, not only in the magic and cabalistic writings of Trithemius, Reuchlin, and Agrippa de Nettesheim but also in Paracelsus' treatises, although he rather deals with them as with conditions of the human fantasy or elemental spirits.

The companion piece to St. Hieronymus is a Stigmatization of

St. Francis which is based on a woodcut by Dürer, with the difference that the figure does not predominate as in Dürer's print, but is submerged by the rich growth of nature. The Saint apparently has just left the forest on his way down to an enchanting valley, while his companion has gone ahead. At this moment, the evening sky flames up in a yellow glare, and in its midst appears the winged Crucified Saviour who marks the Saint with magic rays.

A most enchanting example of the microcosmic concept in painting is a tiny panel of 1507 (Fig. 24, Berlin, Deutsches Museum) which shows a hiding place underneath huge fir trees and a rock wall, where a wild woman enjoys the company of a satyr, a subject represented by Dürer in an engraving.[12] The foliage forms the most delicate color embroidery in golden green, lined by the warm brown of the rock. From this point the eye leaps to the hazy distance, which shimmers in lightest blue and slate green. In the small expanse of the picture surface, the unlimited width of space is caught, together with the dreamy mood of a bright summer day.

In another painting of 1507 (Bremen, Kunsthalle), Altdorfer placed the Nativity of Christ amid the ruins of an old castle covered by freshly fallen snow which gives bluish reflections in the moonlight. Little angels like elemental ghosts make a hubbub in a decaying cornloft, from which they throw down sheaves for the bed of the Infant Saviour. It is the spirit of popular fable, song, and fairy tale created by the people and expressing the people's feeling which distinguishes Altdorfer's type of religious painting. Much of the spirit of folklore is alive in it, ennobled to the rank of high art. This is art truly connected with the soil. When the Holy Family flee to Egypt,[13] they take a rest at a road fountain in the Danube valley, adorned with curious stone deities which resemble gods of the forest. All the picturesque beauties of the country are assembled as if in a treasure box: old towns with walls and gates, crumbling castles, blossoming forests, radiant blue mountain chains. The painter transmits the joy of traveling in a beautiful country to the spectator.

Altdorfer painted the Rest on the Flight into Egypt at a time when he undertook another journey to Austria.[14] These journeys

always meant a new increase in his inventive strength and pictorial mastership, a new bold step forward. From this journey
there is preserved a landscape drawing dated 1511, which represents the Danube valley at Sarmingstein in Upper Austria (Fig.
27). It is an eloquent example of what Altdorfer intended to
convey in his landscapes. The whole picture seems to be in motion. The mountains tower like volcanic eruptions, like fountains
of lava, and seem to bar the way to the water. The buildings
erected by human hands crumble, while aboriginal vegetation
creeps over the new surface of the earth. We seem to witness a
process of geological genesis. Altdorfer's imagination visualized
in his works the creative forces of nature which work beneath the
surface. His landscapes do not give a mere statement of visual
facts; they *express* something.

A more faithful image of reality, as it appears to the eye, was
given by the second great painter of the Danube School, Wolf
Huber, an Austrian from Feldkirch in Vorarlberg, who later settled in Passau as court painter of the bishop.[15] He is the first example of an artist who traveled through the country in order to
make sketches of beautiful places from nature.[16] In an amazing
drawing of 1510 (Fig. 28) he shows the Mondsee in the Salzkammergut, as it still can be seen today — a log bridge and some cut
willows nearby, the Schafberg in the distance. The curving of the
coastline suggests not only depth of space but also the idea of the
curving of the earthly globe under the firmament. It is a faithful
aspect of reality, as perceived by a person from a definite standpoint in this vast expanse of space. With all the meaningful econ-
omy of its line work, Huber's sketch foreshadows more of the
scientific era's approach to nature than Altdorfer's interpretative
drawing.

To uncover the secret forces in nature was also the purpose of
science as represented by Paracelsus. Theophrastus Paracelsus von
Hohenheim, some fifteen years younger than Altdorfer, was born
in 1493 in Switzerland, the descendant of a Swabian family. He
called Austria his second home. He spent many years of his short
life in travel all over Europe, because the spirit of an explorer lived
in him, yet he always found the way back to his native mountains.

His soul was imbued with the spirit of homely nature, and therefore his intellectual formulations were often surprisingly similar to the artistic visions of Altdorfer.

Nature was to Paracelsus a spiritual total which is reflected in every one of its parts. The aboriginal matter was to him the Mysterium Magnum, out of which God shaped the world like an artist. The idea of the artist occurs again and again, and demonstrates Paracelsus' intuitive, artistic approach toward nature. In the act of creation, one substance changes into the other. God created the elements that they may be a matrix for the various substances — for instance, water as a matrix for the minerals, earth as a matrix for wood and plants, ether as a matrix for rain, snow, light, the rainbow and the lightning. One substance merges into the other, opposed to its previous stage, yet bound to it by a deep inner similarity. Paracelsus' ideas on chemistry, largely involved in the adventurous topics of alchemy, are based on speculations of this kind.

Altdorfer painted, about 1511, a monumental panel of St. John the Baptist and St. John the Evangelist (Fig. 26; Regensburg, Museum), for whom he probably used himself and his younger brother Erhard as models, seated in the clearing of a forest, where plants spring up in lush growth in the summer heat. The cosmogonic landscape of the background shows steam rising from the sea, becoming smoke in the height, crystallizing to snowy mountains which dissolve again into wandering clouds. Rocks, cities, ships grow like mineral formations out of the water. In a kind of picture alchemy, one form distills from the other.

Altdorfer would not have been able to visualize the moving forces in nature so well if he had not been such a great painter. His mastery of color was equal to that of Grünewald, yet more as a result of deep contemplation of nature than of mystical vision. He reached the height of his art of color in the large folding altar which he completed in 1518 for the Austrian monastery of St. Florian. The spiritual event of Christ's Resurrection is there depicted as the color miracle of a glorious morning, where the green sky flames up in purple, gold, and sulphur yellow, and the mountains shine forth in lilac hues. A Nativity of Christ which Altdorfer painted about 1520 (Vienna, Kunsthistorisches Museum) renders the Bible story as a cosmic rejoicing, where figures, rocks, and buildings burn in phosphoric colors out of darkness. *Putti* with lanterns throw light circles on the snow, and a circle of light opens in heaven, containing angels like countless globules of light, an assemblage of celestial bodies in the universe, of which our globe is only one small part — an idea which about this time broke through in science in the system of Copernicus.

The frequent references to color in Paracelsus' writings prove that this style of painting was familiar to him. He accepted color as an indication of the proceedings in the atmosphere. To Altdorfer, it was a means of imbuing the narrative with the mood of nature and scenery. The expression of the time of the year and hour of the day was never omitted in his historical paintings.

Albrecht Altdorfer's younger brother Erhard, a less penetrating spirit, rejoiced more in brightly decorative aspects of nature which enhance the splendor of the narrative. He also worked in Austria and painted an altar with the legend of St. Leopold for Kloster-neuburg.[17] A panel showing the Saint who kneels before the miraculous elderbush with the veil formed a part of it (now in the Stiftsmuseum, Klosterneuburg).

Paracelsus' native country, Switzerland, contributed an impor-tant share to the origin of landscape art. There prevailed the spirit of the extraordinary and adventurous, of poetical enhancement, independent of the purpose of religious subject matter. We notice it in a drawing of a tremendous rock mountain by Nikolaus Manuel Deutsch,[18] and in the fantastic portrait of a Swiss lake by Hans Leu,[19] where a rock grows up in the foreground like a thick tree, and the glaciers rise in the background.

Paracelsus called the art of interpretation of nature "chiro-mancy." He applied it not only to the hands of men but also to plants, trees, woods, and finally even to scenery, through the means of mountains, roads, and rivers. The grandest chiromancy of scenery ever achieved by an artist is Albrecht Altdorfer's Battle of Alexander the Great against the Persian King Darius at Issus (Munich, Aeltere Pinakothek) which he painted in 1529 for Duke Wilhelm IV of Bavaria (Fig. 29). It unfolds a cosmic world pan-orama like the maps of the new cosmography. One color flows into the other; the elements fire and water fight in the air like men on earth. The fiery red and orange of the setting sun gilds the peaks of the gentian blue mountains; their chains circumscribe the vault of the earthly globe. The approaching night is illuminated by magic moonlight. Thus, Paracelsus wrote that the firmament is not of one complexion, but of many. In Rueland Frueauf's paintings, one definite local color is given to everything as its attribute. Altdorfer's colors are like those of the elementary substances described by Paracelsus: "They have no definite color, but many colors grow from them; they are composed from many colors." [20]

Altdorfer's contemporary Wolf Huber, whose main importance lies in his excellent landscape drawings, started with intimate motifs, which he treated with topographic exactitude. He considered the most modest things worthy of treatment as main subjects. While in Italy only ideal heroic and saintly figures were considered as worthy subject matter for artistic representation, the Northern draughtsman elevated some willows and an old mill at a creek to the same importance. In his late years, under Altdorfer's influence, Huber went all the way from the intimate to the cosmic. In a drawing of 1541 [21] he unfolds a vast panorama of the globe with lakes, towering peaks, glaciers, and cities. In a drawing of 1552 [22] we face a petrified cosmogony. Flowing masses of lava have crystallized to fantastic mountains covered with pine forests as with a down, and inhabited by cliff-dwellers. There we stand at the threshold of the cosmic landscapes by Bruegel who began his activity about this time.

Altdorfer's development went rather the opposite way. His art concludes with a concentration of the macrocosm to quiet compositions, using motifs from his native world. Then, he took the momentous step of making landscape an end in itself in both painting and prints. In one of his etchings,[23] a monumental old fir tree stretching its branches over the scenery is heroized as the main content of the composition. And in a quiet picture of the Danube valley (Munich, Aeltere Pinakothek), Altdorfer initiates landscape painting in its own right, freed from all religious, historical, and allegorical implications, as a category of painting which was to become predominant in modern art. This painting in its quiet harmony visualizes the same feeling which is contained in a sentence from the *Paradoxa* of the great mystic Sebastian Franck,[24] the continuator of the new pantheistic concept of nature in the realm of philosophical thought: "As the air fills everything and is not confined to one place, as the light of the sun overfloods the whole earth, is not on earth and nonetheless makes all things on earth verdant, thus God dwells in everything, and everything dwells in Him."

IV

Reformation, Humanism, and the
New Notion of Man

ONE of the main factors which contributed not only to the richness of the cultural picture offered by Northern Europe in the sixteenth century but also to its problematic character was the coincidence of religious revolution with artistic and scientific regeneration. This revolution flared up in Italy as well, but only in single symptoms and personalities, from Savonarola to Juan de Valdés, and it did not disrupt the traditional course of religious life, which became reconciled with the development of humanism and artistic renascence. In the North, the demand for reform of religion affected artistic and intellectual life intensely. This demand was finally stronger than all others, especially in Germany.

Humanism and artistic renascence in Northern Europe had their great rise about the same time, at the end of the fifteenth century. Then was laid the foundation of those intellectual and spiritual values which the English word "humanities" and the German word "humanistische Bildung" comprehend. It is inseparably linked with the study of the classical languages. *There are no humanities without the knowledge of Latin and Greek.* This means of course more than memorizing of grammar, syntax, and glossary. It means a new mental attitude toward life. Partial imitation of the classical authors was familiar to the Middle Ages. A true understanding of their personal character as writers came about only at this time. Humanism tried to revive the classical personality and its proper diction. *Thus, it established a new human ideal, based on intellectual culture,* an ideal of spiritual freedom and autonomy of the personality. This is the deeper meaning of that renascence which the Italians called *rináscita.* It is independent of superficial imitation of ancient forms. In Northern

Europe, it means the achievement of a new notion of man as to character and intellectual personality more than anything else.[1]

The new humanistic spirit materialized in the North first of all in those cities which were the doors to the South, open to the infiltration of the new culture: Vienna, Basel, Augsburg. Augsburg formed the artistic and economic bridgehead to Italy. Its commercial rulers, the Fugger family, performed here a task comparable to that of the Medici in Florence. No other German city offers such a Southern aspect as Augsburg; no other was so much imbued with the new Italian Renaissance art. From Augsburg originated the artists who in the most natural and spontaneous way filled Northern art with Southern splendor and the new humanistic spirit: Burgkmair and Holbein. Before Augsburg turned into a Renaissance city, the intellectual culture of humanism had already taken hold of Vienna and Basel. Conrad Celtes, one of the oldest leaders of the new humanistic movement, in 1497 was made by Emperor Maximilian professor of rhetoric and poetry at the University of Vienna. He tried to follow the ancient poets in his epigrams, odes and *Quattuor libri amorum*. As we noticed a new relation to early medieval art about the year one thousand in Dürer's Apocalypse, so Celtes rediscovered early medieval Latinity. He republished the Latin comedies of the nun Hroswitha of Gandersheim. Dürer provided several of his books with title pages and illustrations.[2] Shortly before Celtes died, in February 1508, Hans Burgkmair at his request made a woodcut in his memory (Fig. 31). It shows the poet in half-length, with closed eyes like one of those sleepers on tombstones, his arms crossed on his books. He is framed by an arch, so that the whole composition resembles a Roman epitaph, where the figure of the deceased looks out from a little aedicula. Apollo and Mercury mourn in the spandrels.[3]

The other center of literary humanism was Basel with its busy printing presses. There were published not only the works of ancient poets and philosophers but also of modern satirists. We have already mentioned Sebastian Brant, who belonged to the same generation as Celtes. When Dürer and other young artists illustrated his *Ship of Fools*, they did it essentially in a Late Gothic spirit, notwithstanding many sharp observations of reality. Brant's own caricature, also, as a crazy bibliophile, follows the typical image of the medieval scholar. When Burgkmair in 1508 painted Brant's portrait (Fig. 30),[4] the noble and spirited, lean face appears in a sharply and elegantly cut profile like that on an Italian medal, full of the inner dignity and self-consciousness of the intellectual man. The portrait breathes a new notion of the personality and its value, which is essentially *humanistic*.

Celtes' follower in the professorial chair at Vienna was the young humanist Johannes Cuspinian from Franconia, whose career was extraordinary. At the age of twenty-seven he was rector magnificus of the university. The Emperor awarded him the title "poeta laureatus." His most important work was his book on the Roman Caesars and Emperors which glorifies the German Imperial idea in the light of ancient culture. He was a friend of Lucas Cranach who painted his and his wife's portraits in 1502 (Fig. 32).[5] These paintings have rightly been called the most beautiful Old German portraits. The new positive attitude towards life is expressed in them triumphantly. The young people are embedded in the cosmic totality of nature. Dressed in their most representative attire, they are seated on grassy banks in the open air, amid wild and exuberantly growing vegetation – a feature without any precedent. The twenty-nine-year-old professor wears a solemn academic gown of black velvet and brown fur; his head is covered with a cap of lucid wine-red. Golden curls frame his rosy face which radiates vitality and a firm determination to master the problems which time and the world offer. The bright landscape displays the spell of nature which we know from the early paintings of the Danube School. A rugged oak leads to forests and rising rocks. Manifold life goes on in this scenery, both real and fantastic – washerwomen and bathers at the river, wanderers and hunters, minstrels and dragons in the forest. A star and the professor's astrological bird, the owl, fill the sky. Sidereal and elementary forces entangle man in their magic play. These portraits make visual the pantheistic feeling of the early landscape painters and scientists together with the new humanistic dignity of man. The portrait of Cuspinian's first wife, Anna, sixteen years old, surpasses in brilliancy even that of her husband. Her dress in raspberry-red brocade and black velvet blends with the flowering nature where the elements – ether, fire, water, and earth – rule.

Her childlike face looks almost sullen amidst the display of luminous nature. The paintings apparently were wedding portraits, and as the couple's astrological birds, owl and parrot, also sit in the foliage of the painting of St. Jerome, which we discussed in the last chapter, the latter might have been a wedding gift of the artist.

In a portrait of Cuspinian and his family painted by the Swabian master Bernhard Strigel eighteen years later, in 1520,[6] the scholar has changed very much. He now has two sons, one of them already quite grown up. The enterprising vigor, the storm and stress of the young scholar, have settled down to academic respectability and corporeal stoutness. Agnes Cuspinian, his second wife, is a quiet and watchful Hausfrau, knowing her place at the side of a famous professor. The composition, the lines and colors of this picture, have also been toned down to a quiet balance and lucidity; a single, bare tree remains of the rich landscape. Names of members of the Holy Kindred are written above the persons who adopt saintly roles.

Cranach, recommended by Cuspinian, portrayed also other members of the academic senate of the University of Vienna in the same spirit of human immediacy, merging with nature. The Austrians were always fond of nature. The portrait of Dr. Stephan Reuss, rector magnificus in 1503,[7] does not have the buoyancy of that of his colleague, but a more mature virility, resting in the tranquil light of an afternoon which filters through white clouds in a deep blue sky. An immense warmth pervades this portrait, not only in the gown of deep red cloth lined with brown marten, and in the sunburned complexion, but in the whole feeling of natural, unceremonious humanity as well. The rector's wife [8] reveals the same mature and serene expression of character which is in accordance with the festive raspberry-red and gold of her dress. The broad humanity and earthliness of these portraits, which are worthy heralds of the new century, becomes still more obvious if we compare them with late fifteenth-century portraits. Thoman Burgkmair, Hans Burgkmair's father, painted a wedding portrait of Jakob Fugger the Rich and his beautiful young wife Sibylla Arzt in 1498.[9] It is still full of Gothic ceremoniousness and restraint. Jakob Fugger was the financial dictator of Europe, the economic supporter of the Empire, yet we hardly would guess his tremendous power from the bourgeois decency of this portrait. How much more the personality expands in Cranach's Viennese portraits! It is most revealing to compare this portrait of an Augsburg couple from the end of the Gothic era with another from the end of the High Renaissance era. Hans Burgkmair's pupil Lucas Furtnagel painted in 1527 a portrait of his master and his wife (Fig. 33),[10] full of tragic enervation, bare of the courage of life, based on a scale of black. The faces look out from the picture in sad resignation. Burgkmair's wife holds a mirror in which we notice two death's-heads. The inscription reads as follows: "Such was our shape in life; in the mirror remains nothing but this." The positive spirit and enjoyment of life of the High Renaissance seem to have withered. Man began to think of the beyond again and to consider what the lasting values are. The vanity of things became apparent, yet the flight into the imaginary beyond of the Middle Ages was no longer possible. Life had to be mastered, and the human character had to be proved in it severely and harshly. Life was no longer an artistic performance of the personality, but a duty and task. *The Reformation gave to life this new meaning.* We read it in the stern features of the old Cranach's self-portrait which he painted in 1550.[11] Cranach as an artist became the most faithful exponent of Lutheran Protestantism.

Dr. Christoph Scheurl of Nuremberg, professor of law and rector of the University of Wittenberg, in 1509, the year when Cranach painted his portrait,[12] wrote a panegyric on the artist which is a valuable source for his biography.[13] Lucas Maler, who adopted his name from his native town Cronach in Franconia, was called to Wittenberg in 1504 by Frederick the Wise, Elector of Saxony, to be his court painter. There he came into the very center of the Protestant movement. The painter served Frederick and his followers faithfully for forty-nine years. His portraits of personalities of the Saxon court are numerous. In the beginning, they still keep something of the pictorial spell of the Austrian works, as for instance a woodcut of a Saxon prince riding on a pony through the landscape with Wittenberg in the background, which Cranach did in 1506.[14] Yet the pictorial implements shrunk more and more, and Cranach increasingly concentrated on portraiture as the image of the human character.

Frederick the Wise, portrayed in an engraving by Cranach of 1509,[15] was an upright, pious, and circumspect man, one of the most esteemed and sympathetic figures among the German Electors. After Maximilian's death, he had every chance to be elected as German Emperor, had he felt himself strong enough to master the conflicting forces. Yet he abominated the use of force, and loved to adorn his beautiful country with castles where he gathered magnificent works of art.[16] He was a patron of Dürer in early years, and the master devoted one of his most impressive late portrait engravings to him.[17] The Elector appears there as a pondering, brooding spirit, as a titanic character whose face is shaped mightily in bulging lines. Dürer seems to have lent something of his own struggling spirit to the model. The woodcut by Cranach, Frederick the Wise Praying before the Madonna (Fig. 34),[18] certainly gives a truer picture of this quiet character. Frederick had assembled a huge treasure of relics in his chapel.[19] His homely features reveal sincere piety. His straightforwardness and righteousness made him favor the cause of religious reform. Like Luther, he had a deep veneration for the Holy Writ, and so he became the political sponsor of Luther's fight for the purity of the Word of God.

The likeness of man was always the special strength of Cranach's art. It was a matter of course that the spiritual atmosphere of Protestantism, which centers in the idea of the strength of faith of the individual, was sympathetic to Cranach's talent. Thus Cranach became the portrait painter of the Reformation. He realized in his own life the Protestant ideal of industriousness and sanctification of the working day. In addition to his artistic work, he performed functions in public life as councillor and chamberlain, and finally as burgomaster of Wittenberg. He was a close friend of Dr. Martin Luther whom he portrayed first in an engraving of 1520 as an Augustinian friar.[20] Luther was in this year godfather to Cranach's daughter Anna. The subtle engraving shows the mighty head of the religious fighter, in whom an unbending determination for the cause of the Gospel dwells. The skin stretches over the bony structure of the strong skull which is ready to ram every obstacle. The eyes have a piercing and glowing look. Luther had already published his great early treatises,

An Address to the Nobility of the German Nation, The Liberty of a Christian Man, and *The Babylonian Captivity of the Church.* Justification through belief of the soul confident in the grace of God was to him the essence of religion. Belief is an inner experience which does not need sacred garments, tools, and places as outer tokens. Man has to form Christ in himself. While belief is an invisible process in the human soul, man has to prove his conviction by "doing the work of God in the world." This strong affirmation of the moral personality is the same which speaks with such powerful language in the portraits of Cranach.

When Luther returned from the Diet of Worms in 1521, where he defended his principles, Cranach was the only one whom he informed in a letter about his impending protective custody. We remember how deeply this event stirred Dürer who learned of it in the Netherlands. Luther mentioned Cranach repeatedly in letters which he wrote from the Wartburg. When he came incognito to Wittenberg, armored and bearded as "Junker Jörg," Cranach sketched his portrait and used it for a painting [21] as well as for a vigorous woodcut (Fig. 36).[22]

Luther returned to his public activity in Wittenberg in 1522, against the cautious advice of the Elector. He followed his inner calling. We see him in the portrait which Cranach painted of him in 1526 as a stern and resolute man who has given his fate into the hands of God. Its companion piece is a portrait of Luther's wife Katharina von Bora. These are wedding portraits.[23] Cranach was present as a witness at the wedding feast of the reformer, and when Luther's first son was born, Cranach was his godfather. Cranach and his circle were most faithful followers of Luther. He designed title pages and illustrations for Luther's Reformation pamphlets. His apprentices once even violently clashed with the Catholic students of the university.

To Cranach's most impressive portraits belong those of Luther's parents, kept in the Luther Room of the Wartburg.[24] They were done in 1527 on occasion of a visit of the old people to their famous son in Wittenberg. Luther was from old peasant stock in Thuringia. He wrote: "I am the son of a peasant; my father, grandfather and ancestors were righteous peasants; afterwards my father moved to Mansfeld and became a miner; whence am I."

The old Hans Luther appears here as a father worthy of a great son; he is full of inner vigor and strength, but also of that tremendous harshness and merciless righteousness from which Martin had so much to suffer in his youth. The mother looks like the humble German peasant woman she was, doing her hard daily work as a service to God. Cranach based such carefully executed portraits on water colors and gouache sketches on paper which he did in front of the models. They are much more immediate and alive than the executed panels. A fortunate chance has preserved the sketch of Luther's father (Fig. 35). The author discovered it sixteen years ago and acquired it for the Albertina.[25] The grandeur of the character is here still more impressive. The old man seems to have emerged from the depth of the mountains like an elemental spirit. Something of the pantheistic feeling of the Austrian Cranach portraits awakens here.

There is no doubt that this concentration on a stern picture of the human character meant a certain impoverishment of an art which was in its beginnings rich and imaginative. Protestantism was not favorable to the arts. Moral and ethical values mattered more. We can trace this gradually in Cranach's development.

The wedding portraits of Duke Henry the Pious and Katharina von Mecklenburg of 1514 show festive richness of appearance.[26] Duke Henry of the Albertinian line introduced Protestantism in Dresden and Leipzig. In his early years he was a great collector of huge guns which Cranach designed for him, and which he liked to dust himself. In a later portrait of 1537,[27] all enjoyment of pictorial splendor has gone. We see the old Duke, holding a tremendous sword, a gloomy defender of the evangelic creed. In an early portrait of a young man in the Metropolitan Museum of Art[28] a softly glowing light seems to radiate from the sitter which melts all contrasts into a harmonious pictorial unity. In the portrait of the astronomer and mathematician Dr. Johannes Schöner of 1529,[29] the sitter is seen in hard, clear, almost abstract daylight which reveals the stern character of the man in every wrinkle. The sitters of Cranach's late portraits are neither beautiful nor colorful, but stouthearted people.

Severity may even turn to a certain torpidity as in some of the last portraits of the reformers. It is as if the vivid flow of spirit of the early reform movement had frozen into a new dogmatism. This historical process took place in reality. Protestantism entered its scholastic stage. This was the tragedy of the finest and most humane spirit among the reformers, Philipp Melanchthon.[30] He tried to unite the reformers' religious determination with humanism. He shrank back from all violence, and even sincerely hoped for a unification of all Christian churches. Theology was to him only the means of moralization of human life. Although Protestantism owes to him its first formulation of ethics and dogmatics, the *Loci Communes Rerum Theologicarum*, and the Augsburg Confession, he finally lost all hope because of the "wrath of the theologians" (rabies theologorum). When he died, his last prayer was for peace among the fighting churches. His face, which appears so clear and spiritualized in Dürer's engraving of 1526,[31] looks tired of life in one of Cranach's last portraits, handed down to us in a woodcut.[32] This noble spirit, the follower of Cicero and the Stoics, who achieved an educational work of tremendous importance for the future, who tried to obtain in his thought a clearness similar to that of his favorite master Dürer in his creations, finally broke down under the impossibility of reconciling the ideas of humanity and tolerance with the deep split which had parted the Christian world. Humanism went a different way from Protestant dogmatism and found its noblest artistic expression in other surroundings.

Melanchthon the theologian tried to bring the natural light of the human intellect which shines in the works of the ancient philosophers into historical connection with the teaching of Christ as its fulfillment. Desiderius Erasmus of Rotterdam, the humanist, who started from the ancient writers, tried to penetrate from Cicero, Seneca, and Plato to the "philosophy of Christ." Christ's doctrine was to him the very essence of charity, simplicity, patience, and purity. So the great religious question of the time offered the locus geometricus where the endeavor of the theologian and of the humanist met.

Our idea of Erasmus' personality is insolubly connected with his portraits by Hans Holbein.[33] The first portrait which the artist painted of him (Longford Castle) is dated 1523. The spirited, refined, sceptical features of the scholar are framed by the dark cap and fur-lined gown of a Dutch ecclesiastic. He is slightly turned toward the spectator, yet does not fix his eyes upon him; he keeps aloof and looks into the distance. This is the true Erasmus, always feeling chilly, shrinking back from the hard grip of the world, which he nevertheless dominated intellectually. His surroundings are a classical Renaissance pillar and books, the world of books, so dear to him. His hands rest on a beautifully bound copy of his *Labors of Hercules*. The study for the hands is preserved, subtly done in metalpoint, the technique of most of Holbein's earlier drawings, revealing the bony structure of the scholar's hands which are as eloquent and spirited as Erasmus' features.[34]

Erasmus was then at the height of his fame, the most widely known scholar in the civilized world, comfortably settled in the friendly atmosphere of old Basel, an intimate place, inviting for quiet reflexion, but at the same time a center of the learned world.[35] Erasmus and Holbein had come in contact before, although not personally. Erasmus first came to Basel in 1514, not least attracted by the fact that it was the center of book printing in Northern Europe. It was the printing press which enabled him to keep his intellectual hold on Europe. He collaborated with Badius in Paris and with Aldus Manutius in Venice. Amid the bustle of a printing office, he often found his best time for writing, correcting, and revising texts. In Basel was the outstanding printing press of Johannes Froben. Erasmus' *Adagia*, a collection of proverbial sentences and passages from ancient writers, and his *Praise of Folly* had made his name famous. Now he was anxious to further his edition of St. Jerome's works and the Greek edition of the New Testament. From a classical scholar, Erasmus had increasingly become a religious thinker. This turned all the hopes of Europe toward him. He took up the study of Greek mainly for the purpose of obtaining the documents of Christianity from the sources.

His great talent as a refined and witty writer, however, had not been idle. On his way from Italy to the North, when he crossed the Alps, he had conceived the idea of the *Encomium Moriae*,[36] the *Praise of Folly*, briefly called *Moria*, which he completed in the home of his friend Thomas More in England. In it the great spirit mocks the world and himself, knowing the weakness of all pride, ambition, and success in this world. Folly appears before an audience of fools and asserts that the gods and men owe it only to her if they are happy. She pretends to follow the ancient sophists and to deliver a laudatory oration — yet rather one on herself. She recommends herself to the audience, because she does her job better than the modern sophists, the professors at the universities, who instruct youth only in quarreling. She maintains that at least she is genuine, while the donkey's ears of the so-called wise men peep out in spite of them. A friend of Erasmus, the schoolmaster Oswald Myconius, had his copy of the *Moria* provided with marginal drawings by the brothers Ambrosius and Hans Holbein, done during evening lectures given by Myconius on the *Moria* in winter 1515–16 before young people. In one of the drawings, we see Erasmus himself, fascinated by a pretty girl in the street and stepping into the egg basket of a market woman. Myconius lent his book to Erasmus for his amusement. When the scholar saw this drawing, he sighed and said: "Oh if Erasmus were still so young, he would take a wife immediately."

Hans and his older brother Ambrosius Holbein were the sons of the outstanding painter Hans Holbein the Elder of Augsburg. The stupendous portrait art of the son had its roots in the instruction of the father who drew the most lively likenesses of his contemporaries in silver point sketchbooks. One of the most beautiful is a sketch of his own sons at the age of sixteen and fourteen years (Berlin, Kupferstichkabinett). Ambrosius was an excellent artist, too, as we may conclude from a portrait drawing of a young man dated 1517.[37] Yet his career was broken off before his time — he died about 1519.

Hans Holbein the Younger's first important patron in Basel was the banker Jacob Meyer "zum Hasen." When he was elected burgomaster of Basel in 1516, Holbein painted two marvelous portraits of him and his wife, vigorous images of Swiss Renaissance people, bright and solid, full of burgher pride and unhampered humanity.[38] Burgomaster Meyer also commissioned Holbein's greatest ecclesiastic work, the Madonna for the cathedral of Basel, who protects him and his family, kneeling in ardent prayer.[39] It is a work of classical beauty and harmony. It has the deep lucidity of the paintings of Lombardy which Holbein had seen in 1518, yet is absolutely Northern in sentiment. It is also a document of

religious conviction. It was painted at a time when the disturbances of the Reformation, which became particularly violent in
Basel, began. It was Holbein's last picture before he left for England. Erasmus wrote in a letter to Petrus Aegidius which Holbein
took with him, "Here the arts are shivering with cold." Meyer
belonged to the Catholic party, and confided himself and his family to the protection of the Madonna.

Holbein's drawings for the *Moria* had attracted the attention of
the printer Froben. Beginning in 1516, Holbein became one of
his busiest designers, drawing title pages, initials, borders, and
vignettes in a wonderful Renaissance style, clear-cut and noble
like the Latin phrases of Erasmus.[40] One of them is the title page
to the *Utopia* of Thomas More. We shall discuss later the importance which the English philosopher had for Holbein. Now,
we shall refer briefly to Holbein's relation to the scholars of Basel.
The man who introduced him personally to Erasmus was the
young Bonifacius Amerbach, son of the printer Amerbach, professor of law at the university, later the heir of Erasmus and
founder of the magnificent Holbein collection which is now in
the museum of Basel. Holbein painted his portrait in 1519. The
beautiful and earnest head of the young scholar stands out against
a deep blue sky which is crossed by a few laurel branches and
confined by snowy peaks at the horizon. This is the most harmonious fusion of Italian and Northern Renaissance ever achieved
in painting, a work completely in that humanistic spirit for which
Erasmus' thought stands as a symbol.

Holbein painted two more almost identical portraits of Erasmus
in 1523, one in the Louvre (Fig. 37), the other in Basel, representing him in the attitude of writing. They are of great simplicity
and clearness, showing the head of the scholar in pure profile. He
is completely absorbed in his activity; mocking wrinkles play
around his tight lips. Here we see Erasmus in his favored occupa-
tion of writing, weighing the sentences carefully and without
emotion — the most eloquent humanistic portrait in existence.

During his various sojourns in England, Erasmus had made
friends with many humanists there, especially with Thomas
More,[41] to whom he dedicated his *Moria*. In 1526, when the situation of art in Basel became worse, Holbein left the city for Eng-

land with a letter of introduction to More from Erasmus. In a letter of December 18th, More replied: "Your painter, my dear Erasmus, is a marvelous artist." More had published in 1516 his *Utopia*, the first of a long genealogy of political utopias. More's ideal state on an island establishes the law of religious freedom with the consequence that all religious contrasts merge gradually into one great religion. Belief and immortality are based on reason. The laws of the ideal community are those implanted by God in nature. This religious ideal moves along the same line as that of the reformers, although More was canonized as a holy martyr by the Catholic church. The *Utopia* is full of daring prophecies which later centuries brought to fulfillment. More was a great idealist who fell as a victim of the opposing principles of the time. When Holbein arrived, More's star was rising. The statesman opened to the painter the way into the highest circles of English society. At Christmas 1526, Holbein painted a large group portrait of More's family which was never completed. When Holbein returned to Basel in 1528, he brought along a preparatory pen drawing (Fig. 39) as a gift for Erasmus who expressed in a letter of thanks his joy in being reunited with his friends in effigy at least.[42] This important work is the first example of a type of painting which reached its climax in the seventeenth century in the works of Frans Hals and Rembrandt. The family is grouped in an English drawing room around More and his father, who are seated. Holbein was as great a draughtsman as a painter. A series of magnificent portrait drawings in colored chalks for this group portrait are preserved in the Library of Windsor Castle. In them we see the delicate features of Anne Cresacre, the sixteen-year-old daughter-in-law who appears behind More in the picture.[43] An open and intelligent look characterizes Cecily Heron, the twenty-year-old daughter seated at her father's feet.[44] And the lively features of an old gentleman, full of vitality and English bonhomie, are those of the grandfather John More, judge of the King's Bench.[45]

To the circle of Erasmus' humanistic friends belonged some prominent members of the English clergy whose portraits have come down to us in paintings and drawings by Holbein. John

Colet,[46] Dean of St. Paul's, was one of his intimates. He was a universally cultured man who lectured on the letters of the Apostle Paul at Oxford University. John Fisher,[47] Bishop of Rochester, was the man who together with More suffered the death of a martyr for his faith, beheaded in 1535 by the order of King Henry VIII. Erasmus intended to dedicate to him one of his last works, the *Ecclesiastes*. William Warham,[48] the archbishop of Canterbury, tried ardently to tie Erasmus to England by awarding him the rectory of Aldington. Holbein also painted a portrait of Nicholas Kratzer,[49] the court astronomer to Henry VIII, a Bavarian from Munich, who had met Dürer in Erasmus' house in the Netherlands. Kratzer was an adherent of the Reformation in Germany and corresponded with Dürer on scientific and religious matters.

When Holbein returned in 1528 to Basel, he found his family in economic distress. The wonderfully expressive portrait which he painted of his wife and his two children on this occasion (Basel), shows their faces tired and saddened. Remarkably enough, a certain affinity to Grünewald can be noticed in this work. The religious turmoil in Basel was at its height then. The iconoclastic tendency of Protestantism took the upper hand. The mob stormed the churches and destroyed all works of religious art. Erasmus wrote, "Nothing has survived, neither in the cloisters nor on the portals, nor in the convents. The pictures were covered with white-wash; what could burn was thrown on the bonfire, the rest was smashed. Neither monetary nor artistic value was any protection." Holbein himself followed the new creed only reluctantly, not from inner conviction. He belonged to those persons summoned by the city council in June 1530 because of their abstaining from the Protestant service and communion. He gave as reason that he needed a better explanation of the communion before he would go to it.[50]

Erasmus moved to Freiburg, so much was he disgusted by the events in Basel. Freiburg belonged to the Catholic house of Austria, and the Archduke Ferdinand gave a letter of protection to Erasmus. He did not have to fear a repetition of the Basel events in Freiburg. Protestantism was on the way to turning Germany into a cultural desert. Erasmus complained, "Wherever Lutheranism rules, the study of the humanities slackens." And Luther thundered against him in his table talks as an "enemy of all religion and especial adversary of Christ, a complete likeness of Epicure and Lucianus." Reformation won the battle over humanism completely. We know how much the backbone of German art was broken for the rest of the century, in spite of ingenious talents. In these surroundings, an artist of Holbein's dimensions could not stay any longer. His art belonged to the world. He returned in 1532 to London.

In 1530, before Holbein left Basel for good, he portrayed Erasmus in his new home at Freiburg. The panel formerly in the Pierpont Morgan Collection (Fig. 38) shows the old humanist, once the preceptor of Europe, in a black garb on simple blue ground, his features sharpened, worn out by a laborious and troublesome life. The little roundel in the Basel museum presents the same features, yet radiant from a faint inner light — the light of the intellect whose flame burned in Erasmus unslackened. He saw clearly the spiritual and religious demands of his time, yet he shrank back from the radical conclusions which Luther drew, and did not dare break with the old church. His humanistic spirit, fond of tranquility, harmony, and balance, detested violence.[51] The death of his friends More and Fisher threw dark shadows on his soul. His position is comparable to that of Melanchthon on the Protestant side whom Holbein portrayed at the same time in a similar miniature painting (Hannover, Provinzialmuseum). As Melanchthon's end was overshadowed by the hopelessness of reconciling the fighting churches, so the sceptical look of the old Erasmus seems to penetrate the vanity of all efforts to conquer the Kingdom of Heaven with fire and sword.

Holbein's last Erasmus portrait is a woodcut which appeared in 1540 after the scholar's death in the edition of Erasmus' works. It is a kind of printed epitaph for the humanist. Erasmus im Gehäus stands in the doorway of a rounded Renaissance arch, leaning on his symbol, the herma of Jupiter Terminus. Alexander Stewart once presented to Erasmus a ring with an ancient gem representing Terminus. Hence, Erasmus chose the Terminus for his emblem, and used the stone as a seal. He connected the Terminus with the idea of the limit of all things. Thus Terminus reminded him of the end of life. There, he looks back from behind his symbol. Terminus in the woodcut indicates the end not only of Erasmus' life but also of his epoch of culture, one of the greatest in European history.

V

The Pictorial Unity of Late Gothic and Renaissance

The Masters of the Netherlands

IT IS one of the peculiarities of the German nation that it is always inclined to break off a course of development and enter a new one, throwing overboard the highest achievements previously gained. Hence the sudden changes, the irrational leaps, the catastrophic turns which we find so often in German history. This is also reflected in the fine arts. We remember what the mature Dürer thought of the works which impressed him in his youth.

The flow of development is much steadier in the Western countries, especially in the Netherlands. Because of their extensive international relations, the Netherlands took up the new discoveries and new trends more speedily than any other country of Northern Europe. Nevertheless, Dutch and Flemish painting of the Renaissance descends in a broad and uninterrupted stream from Old Netherlandish painting of the dying Middle Ages. Pictorial culture reached a height in the Netherlands during the fifteenth century which it had attained nowhere else. A stronger sense of tradition seems to have kept the Dutch and Flemish artists from breaking with the past as radically as the Germans did. I wish to illustrate this with a few examples.[1]

The leading German painter-engraver in the second half of the fifteenth century was Martin Schongauer, whose works impressed the young Dürer so strongly that he desired to become his pupil. Schongauer's best authenticated panel painting, The Madonna in the Rose Arbor of 1473 in Colmar, is the perfect embodiment of the Late Gothic idea of the Virgin. In spite of a balanced composition and emphasis on main accents, it is filled with the restless movement characteristic of the mode of the time. Draperies and garments are in motion; folds creep and contours flutter. The forms are brittle and spiny. Naturalistic observations in details like faces and hands, which have a strongly German flavor, far from Southern beauty, and in birds and flowers, which are set off against an abstract gold ground, do not impair the design- and patternlike character of the whole. Everything is based on expressive lines; pictorial values are almost less obvious than in Schongauer's engravings.

Thirty years later, Dürer, in Venice, painted the Virgin with the Siskin.[2] The subject matter is the same: the Madonna crowned by angels and the child enjoying birds and flowers. But what a tremendous change. The triangular composition is now realized by full round solids. The ponderous figure of Mary fills the picture space; her contours encompass the children. All Gothic brittleness has gone. Hands have a firm grasp. Heads are spheres, and faces show a typical ideality. The Virgin sits before a brocaded reredos in a luminous scene as in a painting by Bellini. The brilliant light enlivens the coloring and the plasticity of all things. Within a short time, artistic aims and ideas have changed to the contrary in almost every respect.

In the Netherlands the artists who played the role of the initiators of the Renaissance, as did Dürer in Germany, were Massys and Gossaert. In the following pages we shall compare some of their works with considerably earlier examples of Netherlandish painting. Jan van Eyck's Madonna in the Church (Fig. 40),[3] painted in the 1430's, shows the figure of the Virgin superhuman in size, but nevertheless most tender and graceful, standing in the main nave of a Gothic cathedral. Sunbeams fall through the tracery of the windows and bathe the whole in the most wonderful poetry of light. Light and colors form a unity which is as real as possible, yet full of the mood of a holiday, of blessed seclusion. Angels in the vestments of deacons fulfill their duties before the burning candles of the High Altar in the choir. The Madonna seems to be a materialization of the hallowed atmosphere of this sacred building.

About seven decades later, Quentin Massys painted his Madonna in the Church (Fig. 41; Count Antoine de Seilern Collection).[4] Elements of the Renaissance style, similar to those in late paintings by Memling, have infiltrated the architecture. The decorative splendor of the representation has also increased, but, with different means, the painting still tries to express the same spirit as Van Eyck's work. The Virgin appears as Queen of Heaven in lucid garments which in exuberant flow cover her subtle figure. With the angel children who make themselves pleasant to the shy babe, a new note of festive gayness has entered, yet, through the round arch, still we look into the choir of the silent church where angels prepare the throne for the arrival of the Madonna and range themselves with torches for the solemn procession.

Hans Memling, the leading master of the Bruges school of painting in the second half of the fifteenth century, painted an altarpiece for Sir John Donne of Kidwelly [5] in the 1460's where music making angels and the family of the donor, introduced by their patron saints, kneel in Gothic solemnity around the enthroned Madonna. The quiet Flemish landscape in the background does not disturb but rather enhances the grave and devout mood of the pillarlike figures which surround the Virgin in symmetrical composition.

Jan Gossaert painted the Malvagna Triptych in the museum of Palermo for an Italian patron after 1511. He had been in Italy from 1508 to 1509. No trace of the Southern grandeur and monumentality, which the artist had experienced shortly before, can be found in the triptych. The Madonna still sits in an open hall with outlook on an idyllic scene, surrounded by an angelic orchestra. Although the angels are now half nude little *putti* instead of shy children in long garments, the mood of holidaylike seclusion has not changed. The solemn, aristocratic forms of Memling's architecture have become a precious lacework of stone and metal, yet no signs of Southern Renaissance forms can be noticed in this sparkling embroidery of Late Gothic Flamboyant architecture. The restless swings and curves have even seized the frame, so that it sweeps in keel arches. The precious, jewel-like perfection of fifteenth-century paintings is maintained. The feeling of aloofness from the loud, profane world is even stronger in the two wings where St. Catherine and St. Dorothy, seated in the garden of their *Beguinage*, devote themselves to quiet meditation, not distracted by their little assistants who turn the pages of the book or urge them to make flower wreaths. The artist retained the Late Gothic world of forms on purpose, and was intent upon continuing the old tradition, although the outsides of these wings reveal that he already knew of Dürer's Renaissance discoveries.

Although Dürer was greatly indebted to Schongauer, his immediate predecessor in the sequence of time, there was a mental break between them, a cleavage, which indicates two different eras of mind. The period which elapsed between Van Eyck and Massys lasted much longer, three quarters of a century, yet nowhere do we feel the presence of such a break. One great flow of unified development seems to connect the masters at the beginning and at the end of that great chapter of Western painting, without the change of the basic mental attitude. Even Massys' harking back to the "heroic" phase of Old Netherlandish painting, to Van Eyck, Petrus Christus, the Master of Flémalle, and Rogier van der Weyden, appears not so much as a protest against the unheroic art of the immediate past, the Late Gothic, as in Dürer's Apocalypse and in the glowing professions of Grünewald, but rather as the harmonious conclusion of a development which followed its own rhythm.

Netherlandish art kept an autonomous role. Although the Netherlands were torn as much as Germany by political, intellectual, and religious strife during the sixteenth century, they never swept art so radically from the stage as the German speaking countries did. The phase of transition between two great epochs produced here works of art which are fascinating not so much as creations of single outstanding personalities but as documents of a high and manifold artistic culture.

Although the Netherlands were, in the era with which we have to deal, a political unit ruled by Emperor Maximilian I as the husband of Mary of Burgundy, the national differentiation of the Southern Netherlands, Flanders, from the Northern Netherlands, Holland, is evident, regardless of frequent overlappings and fusions. In Flanders, the old centers of painting Bruges and Louvain yielded their rank to Antwerp, the economic and cultural center of the country, and to Brussels, the seat of the court. In Holland, the city schools of Haarlem, Delft, and Leiden, which were of basic importance for the art of the seventeenth century, began to develop their characteristics. Yet Netherlandish art was not confined to the area of the Netherlands. The Italian Renaissance during the fifteenth century was limited to Italy, while the Netherlandish style ruled all over Europe. This international recognition makes it necessary for us to seek some of the masters who lead over from the old to the new mode, outside the Netherlands.

When Dürer visited in Malines Vrouw Margaret of Austria, daughter of the Emperor, stadholdress of the Netherlands, she showed him a set of forty small panels in oil colors; he wrote in his diary that he had never seen anything purer and finer in quality. The panels which impressed him so deeply represent the life of Christ and the Virgin, and were painted by Juan de Flandes, court painter to Isabella of Castile.[6] The cycle was called the "Oratory" of Isabella. It is preserved partly in the Royal Palace in Madrid, partly in other European museums. If we look at Christ and the Samaritan Woman in the Louvre, we see a work equally distinguished by nobility of composition, delicacy of design, and refinement of colors. Christ's figure rises tall and slender like the post of the draw-well and the trees in the background. The woman is drawn in subtle and smooth curves, full of a childlike grace. The design is of goldsmith-like perfection, the color of a soft and iridescent lucidity. Wonderful is the effect of space, the wide expanse of air behind the figures, where bare Spanish hills and mountains die away in a haze of light. Juan de Flandes had worked since 1496 for Isabella and died in Palencia in 1519, so his art was hardly any influence on his home country, but it spread the fame of the Netherlands abroad. His panel paintings are of that jewel-like perfection which we admire in the Flemish book illuminations about 1500. One of the masterworks of Flemish book painting is the *Hortulus Animae* in the National Library in Vienna.[7] The giant St. Christopher lifts the Infant Saviour from a rocky coast. The shadows of night fall on the country. A last afterglow illuminates the sky. In the foreground, fishermen carry on with their work by torchlight. A perfect unity of light and atmosphere fills the picture with the mood of nature. The book painters were always pioneers in the observation of reality.

Juan de Flandes was also an excellent painter of portraits. He portrayed members of the royal family. Some of the rare examples of his portrait art came as property of the House of Hapsburg to the Museum of Vienna.[8] The author was so fortunate as to recognize another example in a hitherto anonymous Flemish portrait from an American private collection, which is now deposited in the Fogg Museum of Art. It represents a princess of the Royal Family, perhaps the younger sister of Joanna the Mad (Fig. 43), Catherine of Aragon, later married to Henry VIII of England.[9] The portrait is full of the same grace and nobility which we admire in the panels of the Oratory. It renders perfectly the character of a little girl who is still an innocent child, but already somewhat conscious of the blue blood in her veins and her royal dignity. These are high points of Netherlandish painting, in the best international tradition of Old Netherlandish court art which ruled European taste for one century.

Juan de Flandes' collaborator at the Oratory was another artist of Flemish origin, Miquel Zittoz, known as Master Michiel. Master Michiel's own career was a completely international one. He was court painter to Isabella from 1480 to 1504. After that, he worked at the courts of England, Denmark, and of Margaret of Austria in the Netherlands. His art competes in highest pictorial refinement and delicacy with that of Juan de Flandes, yet gives up Juan's Gothic brittleness and introduces a more Renaissance-like roundness and smoothness. He painted an admirable diptych for a nobleman of the suite of Catherine of Aragon who was a patron of the artist during his sojourn in England. The left portion, in the Museum of Berlin, shows the Madonna with the Child behind a parapet covered by an Oriental carpet; the right portion, in the National Gallery in Washington, represents the donor in prayer before the Virgin (Fig. 42). The nobleman portrayed stands out in matchless perfection from the dark ground. The way the blue brocade of his dress fits into the silvery color chord of the whole is unforgettable. (See Addendum, p. 161, below.)

Another outstanding Netherlandish master of the transitional period is to be found in the Rhineland. Jan Joest van Calcar was already a citizen of Calcar by 1480.[10] This part of Germany was then considered almost as a part of Holland. Dutch was the language of the sermons. Jan Joest spent the last years of his life in

Haarlem, and if he is connected with any Netherlandish school, it is that of Haarlem. Yet his works traveled far, even to Spain; an altar by him is in the Cathedral of Palencia. His main work is the large altar in the Church of St. Nicholas in Calcar with the Life of Christ which he painted between 1505 and 1508. Severity and monumentality are its basic note. The figures are slender and tall, measured in their movements. These are characteristics which we also find in the School of Bruges, for instance in the later works of Gerard David. While the School of Bruges slightly petrifies in its own perfection, Jan Joest prevents this through the soft and melting atmospheric character which he lends to his pictures. His solemnity is quite at ease, and the figures move with natural grace and dignity. The scene of Christ and the Samaritan Woman is not only full of solemnity but also of a quiet poetry in the dreamy atmosphere of a peaceful landscape. The Dutch pictorial element appears as the more modern and progressive one about 1500. We shall learn more about its importance.

The center in which all the various trends from the North and South Netherlands intercrossed was Antwerp. The most famous artist of the generation born around 1460, who were mature men when the decisive turn took place, was Quentin Massys. His fame reached legendary height, especially as legend shrouded his life. He was said to have been first a blacksmith. His house in Antwerp, filled with paintings, was a sight shown to Dürer when he visited the country. His art reveals a great and monumental vein, and is pervaded by a humanistic spirit. Massys was a friend of the humanists Petrus Aegidius and Erasmus of Rotterdam whose portraits he painted in 1517. We know this from a letter of Thomas More, to whom the portraits were sent as a gift. Massys also made a medal of Erasmus. Massys was from Louvain, and enrolled in 1491 as Master in the list of painters in Antwerp, the famous Liggeren, which contain so many valuable documents on the fine arts. We have already noticed in the Madonna in the Church, an early work, Massys' strong inclination toward medieval solemnity. A work in the same style is the serious, almost somber, Madonna on a Gothic throne in the Museum of Brussels, a picture which tenaciously clings to everything traditional in Flemish painting; it is built up in steeply rising verticals. This panel was painted

before the work on the large folding altars — which covers the
years from 1507 to 1511 — began. About 1520, Massys took the
subject up again in the Madonna in the Kaiser Friedrich Museum
in Berlin. The medieval gloom has turned into Renaissance-like
gayness and radiancy. The Virgin happily kisses the nude child
who no longer ponders over the prayer book. A delicious still life
is displayed on the table. The elements of Flamboyant Gothic
still dominate the architecture, yet they contribute to the festive
gayness and lead one's glance to the splendor of the distant scenery.
The type of the Holy Virgin reveals the kind of art Massys has
become acquainted with in the meantime: the art of Leonardo da
Vinci and his Lombard followers. We also see this clearly in
Massys' portraits. The Man with the Carnation in the Art Institute of Chicago is completely in line with the portraits of the
masters of the fifteenth century, Van Eyck and his followers. Its
attitude is restrained and archaic, appropriate to a man who is used
to prayer. The portrait of a Canon in the Liechtenstein Gallery in
Vienna frees the man completely from the scheme of straight
lines, and lets him expand in corporeal plenitude before a vast
sweep of landscape. His look is proud and determined.

   Such contrasts are apt to induce us to see there the progress of
a mature master brought up in the Gothic tradition to the new
Renaissance mode. It would be wrong, however, if we were to
base a chronology of the works of the master on such considera-
tions. We find a work with the date 1514 which is as Gothic in
sentiment as it can be — The Banker and His Wife in the Louvre.
The gloom of people who dwell in somber old houses in the
shadow of Gothic cathedrals speaks to us from this painting.[11] The
dark paneled walls seem to swallow the light. The woman turns
the pages of an illuminated prayer book and looks with a melancholy expression at the man who does his work of weighing gold
as ceremoniously as if it were a religious rite. He is a banker of
the type of Arnolfini and Portinari who had themselves portrayed
by Van Eyck and Van der Goes. The half-length figure of St.
Magdalen in the Museum of Antwerp is hardly later than the
Louvre painting, yet it shines forth with all the delicate splendor
of which a High Renaissance painting of the Netherlands is capable. The color scale is of unsurpassable refinement. The brownish

hue of the skin is almost as light in value as the deep blue sky; the silk of the garment changes between carmine and olive. The painting has a floating texture of colors, and is of a lightness which was not accessible to the painters of the fifteenth century.

The color scale perhaps distinguishes Massys' paintings most from the great works of the fifteenth century, which they emulate so strongly. The tragic grandeur of Rogier van der Weyden's Deposition from the Cross, which Massys saw in his native city Louvain, inspired him when he painted the central piece of the great altar for the Cathedral of Antwerp from 1508 to 1511 at the order of the carpenters' guild (Fig. 44). The kindred and the disciples of Christ attend to the Holy body which is extended in front. The lines of arms and heads describe great arches and triangles concentrating the group in a solemn and monumental chord. But the colors are different from the sculptural simplicity of the old model. A fluctuating richness is spread over the panel, an iridescence of changing tones which reveals a new spirit, more advanced in material and psychological texture. The work is more complicated and, therefore, less striking than those of the great founders of the Flemish School. The same fluctuating richness dominates the rocky scenery where the tomb, illuminated by candles, opens. The two holy senators are figures of as much pomp as dignity and piety. If anything in Netherlandish art can be compared with Grünewald's monumental altars, it is this triptych. Here also we notice a similar modernity and indebtedness to the past blended into one. Of course, Massys remains aloof from Grünewald's radical expressionism. The whole offers almost the glittering aspect of a tapestry. We know little of the early activity of Massys between 1491 and 1507. It seems to have been devoted more to the designing of tapestries than to painting. Tapestry and stained glass had in the Northern countries the same function and importance which fresco had in Italy. A group of Flemish tapestries from about 1500, widely spread over ecclesiastic Europe in magnificent specimens, shows so strongly Massys' style that his artistic energies seem to have been invested first in this branch of monumental art. The iridescence of colored and golden threads continued later in his altar works.

For the church of St. Peter in Louvain, Massys painted in the years from 1507 to 1509 the altar devoted to St. Anne which shows the Holy Kindred in the central piece (Fig. 45). It has nothing in common with the medieval grandeur of the Antwerp altar, although it is the earlier work. A serene balance and harmony ennobles the group which is arranged in a domed Renaissance hall. It is the perfect Northern counterpart to the festive and bright *santa conversazione* of the Italians. The color chord is of diaphanous lightness. That the master was also capable of progressive boldness is proved by the composition of the wings. The Death of St. Anne presents the corner of a narrow bedroom into which the canopy bed with the strongly foreshortened lying figure is squeezed. Mary and Christ as a young boy assist St. Anne. It is astounding how the figure composition is adapted to the narrowness and closeness of the room section. The figures grow in impressive climax towards the spectator. In another wing St. Joachim receives the message of the angel in a mountainous scenery. The way in which his monumental figure kneels down, in which the faithful dog is fitted into the corner, reveals the same sense of compact compositional arrangement. Everything is very naturalistic, but at the same time there is an aery lightness and caressing softness of modeling, pervaded by light and atmosphere. Rubens' altarpieces seem to be foreshadowed in these amazing works.

In a small panel in the Prado at Madrid, Massys has placed a figure group of the Temptation of St. Anthony in gracefully swinging curves before a wide landscape which is the work of Joachim Patenier. The painter, who came from Dinant, worked from 1515 to 1524 in Antwerp. He had friendly relations with many of his famous contemporaries. His main field was landscape painting. The figures, often inserted by other artists, play a secondary role in his pictures. Patenier was not the originator of the panoramic world landscape, because Hieronymus Bosch preceded him in this field, but he was the artist who raised this type of ideal landscape painting to an end in itself. The world is spread out like a map. The planes recede in the sequence of brown, green, and blue, a formula of landscape which was valid until the seventeenth century. It is the landscape appropriate to the era of a new cosmography which is not limited to a small area of known territory, but encompasses the whole globe. The physical world, unlimited according to the new experiences, was presented in its exotic aspects. The fantastic scheme of the "world landscape" was chosen for this purpose, as we may see in a picture of the Conquest of America, ordered by Margaret of Austria from her court painter, the Dutchman Jan Mostaert.[12]

With these artists, we approach a younger generation, that of the men who were independent masters in the first years of the new century and established as members of the guild. They were born in the late 1470's. In 1503 Jan Gossaert and Jan van Leyen were recorded as members of the guild, and in 1504 Jan de Beer. We have already dealt briefly with Jan Gossaert. He originated from the Southern, Franco-Flemish part of the country. His family was from Maubeuge in the Hainault, hence his cognomen Mabuse. We have mentioned before that he had been in Italy in 1508. He was the first Netherlandish artist who studied ancient remains with a newly arisen interest. A drawing of his after an ancient sculpture is preserved.[13] With this study began something completely new in Netherlandish art. We have seen that it did not radically change Gossaert's mode, and that several years later he painted the Malvagna Triptych in the Flamboyant Gothic style. Both ways continue, parallel to each other, frequently blending. Yet the classical mode grew in importance, and gradually, not abruptly, replaced the Late Gothic. The final consequences do not appear with Gossaert himself, but with younger artists. The organism of the picture as a total remains much linked up with Gothic principles, as we may see in Gossaert's famous Lucas Altar in the Rudolphinum at Prague. It was not Italy that caused Gossaert's decided turning toward the new mode, but the overwhelming impression of the art of Dürer. Neptune and Amphitrite, painted in 1516, a composition thoroughly provided with Renaissance elements, follows Dürer's engraving Adam and Eve as model. So it is through a Northern medium that the Southern Renaissance is transmitted.

In the beginnings, Gossaert was strongly rooted in the Old Netherlandish tradition. The Adoration of the Magi in London is a ceremony in the restrained ecclesiastic style of the fifteenth century, composed from verticals which have the rhythm of a solemn choir or procession. The heritage of the masters of the fifteenth century, of Memling and the School of Bruges, is obvious. There is plenty of the study of reality in this painting. Yet these naturalistic observations, combined with a remarkable study of light, remain faithful to the approach toward nature which we see in the paintings of Hugo van der Goes and of the book illuminators. Gossaert himself was entrusted with a task of this kind. He collaborated in the illumination of the famous Breviarium Grimani, ordered by Antonio Siziliano; his name is found as a signature on one of the paintings adorning the manuscript.[14] The pictures of the Breviarium keep the naturalistic heritage of the masters of the fifteenth century, mainly in the calendar illustrations; ornaments and architecture are in Flamboyant Gothic. As this manuscript was painted after Gossaert's return from Italy, it proves that the Late Gothic style was not at all out of fashion then. On the contrary, Flamboyant Gothic was as much modern and timely as the Italian Renaissance mode. Gossaert not only started in this style, but even cultivated it for a considerable while. A clair-obscure drawing in the Albertina,[15] which represents the enthroned Madonna with Saints, is built up from gracefully fluttering curves, swings, leaps and flares, restlessly twisting and turning. This is in every respect the contrary of what we understand by Renaissance repose and balance. It rather seems to be a climax of the inherent tendencies of Late Gothic in its very last phase. Another work of this kind by Gossaert is a project for a large stained glass window with the story of St. John. We have mentioned before that in the North glass painting, like tapestry weaving, replaced the task of monumental wall painting. Almost all the Netherlandish artists were active in this branch of art, including Gossaert. An example in the collection of the Uffizi in Florence has been overlooked by the students of the field, and is unknown so far. Reproduced below (Fig. 47) is the section of the large window which represents St. John stepping into his own tomb.

Gossaert does not stand alone in this tendency. He is only one of the earliest representatives of a considerable group of artists who worked mainly in Antwerp. They are called the Antwerp Mannerists or also the masters of the Bles group, because a painting by one of them, an Adoration of the Magi in Munich, was for some time, on the basis of a forged signature, wrongly attributed

to the landscape painter Herri met de Bles.[16]   The artists of the
Bles group were active in the first quarter of the sixteenth century.
Their activity reached its climax about 1520.

The attitude of scholars toward this group differs. Some of
them use the word "manneristic" in a depreciatory sense. Others
try to save the artists from the reprimand of being mannered and
to attribute positive qualities to their works by calling them representatives of Late Gothic.[17] Yet their Flamboyant is very different from the fifteenth-century Flemish Gothic. It is an absolutely
modern style, and we may well compare its sophisticated refinement of form with the tendencies of the first Italian Mannerists
which were formulated most strikingly by Pontormo in his frescoes of the Certosa di Galuzzo.[18] A positive valuation of this art
is not only possible, but even necessary with regard to the understanding of Netherlandish art of the sixteenth century. The compositions of the Mannerists seem to have lost all physical weight,
like the Beheading of St. John by the Master of the Munich Adoration.[19] The figures move and turn in complicated twists; they
screw themselves up vertically like the bizarre, gracile towers of
the palaces in the background which are neither Gothic in the strict
sense nor Renaissance, but an unprecedented blending of both.

We know the most refined of those Antwerp artists by name,
Jan de Beer, who became master in 1504. He created the splendid
altarpiece of the Adoration of the Magi in Milan. The surface of
the panels is a fantastic turmoil of flaming, flickering forms. Not
a single spot in them permits one to rest and breathe. The eye is
immediately carried away by new currents of movements. The
character of all this movement is irrational, fantastic, imaginative.
The master likes to enhance it with iridescent colors and weird
light effects which have a similar unsteady, will-o'-the-wisp quality. Representations of the Nativity (Fig. 46) [20] give him the
chance to unfold such magic which spotlights here a face, there
a wing, yonder a fluttering sash, while the connecting parts are
plunged into darkness. We are reminded of Altdorfer's magic of
light, yet his naïve spirit of fairy tale is absent.

That the "Renaissance" style of the mature Gossaert always
preserved something of the restless movement of the Mannerists,
we may see in the beautiful drawing of Adam and Eve in the Al-

bertina,[21] where the complete and rational mastery of the nude body did not hinder the artist from indulging in similar complicated interlacements and motions. What importance the preservation of the Gothic heritage through the Mannerists had for later phases of the art of the sixteenth century we shall discuss later. We have now to investigate its sources and origins.

Jan van Leyen, who was listed as master in Antwerp in the same year as Gossaert, came, as his registration reveals, from the city of Leiden in Holland. His real name was Jan de Cock. He was a representative of the Flamboyant style of the Mannerists. Yet the way in which he handles it differs from the Flemings. His works first of all are intended to *narrate*, to tell us a story in that lively and striking manner which was connected with religious art in Holland after the middle of the 15th century. There is nothing merely decorative and ornamental in the little painting of St. Christophorus [22] who carries the Infant Saviour over the swollen river (Fig. 50). We feel how painfully the Saint drags along with his burden which means the whole world. His back bends in such a tremendous curve that his cloak floats on the water. The inhospitable shores are washed out by the flood. A huge whale has been stranded, and an antlike host of people makes use of it. Such an event happened in 1520 when Dürer was in the Netherlands, and he regretted very much that the whale had got afloat again before he could reach the place. The tree with the hut of the Saint twists like a living animal. There, the curves have a deeply expressive meaning like the growth of the wilderness in another painting in which the Saints Paul and Anthony dwell.[23] The raven which has delivered the bread to the astonishment of the Saints takes to the air again with an elegant skip like a plane. The forest goes to seed like the vegetation in the paintings by Altdorfer, yet it is not a homely forest, a faithful picture of reality; it is an imaginary one, as it might appear in dreams.

Where this bewitched vegetation, this spellbound world of sweeping, creeping shapes derives from becomes obvious in a woodcut by Jan de Cock of the Temptation of St. Anthony, dated 1522. There, demons and specters leap forth from the parabolic curves, and make unholy the idyllic surroundings to the holy man. It is the fantastic and demonic world of Hieronymus Bosch which the Dutchman Jan de Cock transplanted from his native country to Flanders. In Bosch's work we meet the temptations of saints where everything assumes spookish life. In Bosch's paintings of the Passion of Christ (Fig. 48) we see the flaming, flickering rhythm of crowded masses. This rhythm, which later became a brilliant firework in the paintings of the Antwerp Mannerists, has there a deeply expressive meaning.

Dutch art of the late fifteenth century, in spite of its tremendous height of pictorial mastership, had as its chief aim not perfection of craftsmanship and naturalistic observation of the Flemings, but expression. The same subjective religious spirit which brought about the mystical movements of the Brothers of the Common Life and the Congregation of Windesheim fills the works of the Dutch painters, whether they go in a realistic direction, like Geertgen tot Sint Jans, or in a fantastic and visionary one, like Bosch. Both are equally expressive, and frequently blend. The Deposition from the Cross by a pupil of Geertgen of Haarlem [24] applies to the figures, seen in the clearness of the open air, a flaming pattern of expressive curves which betray a deeply emotional spirit. The painters of the School of Delft went further in this respect than any others. The Throne of Mercy in the Strossmayr Gallery at Zagreb (Fig. 49) was painted by the strange Master of the Virgin among the Virgins, an anonymous artist of the Delft School. God the Father holds the dead Christ. The Virgin, fainting in the arms of St. John, and the Marys attend as if it were a Crucifixion. Angels with the instruments of the Passion assist. The mournful scene is full of inner dramatic tension. The curving forms move as in a somber, ghostlike dance in the greyish half-light. The types are repellently ugly, almost degenerate. Christ looks like a gipsy. Why did the artist show a saintly scene in such a realistic and at the same time eerie way? Because the ugly and tortuous often voices the language of the soul more clearly than the beautiful and conventional. We find related trends in the popular mystic literature, for instance in the sermons of Jan Brugman who compared Jesus to a drunkard. "Oh, was He not truly drunk, when love urged Him to descend from the highest heavens to this lowest valley of the earth?" [25]

This expressive quality of Dutch Flamboyant Gothic continued into the sixteenth century, when the current split into a Dutch and a Flemish branch. In Holland it continued mainly in the School of Leiden whence came Jan de Cock, who brought this style to Antwerp. Jan de Cock has many features in common with Cornelis Engelbrechtsen, who painted about 1506 the triptych of the Crucifixion for the monastery Marienpoel. It is crowded with slender figures in hectic, curved motion. A little triptych of the Crucifixion by Jan de Cock in the Rijksmuseum at Amsterdam reveals how close the artists were to each other. And Engelbrechtsen was the master of Lucas van Leyden, the greatest Dutch artist of the sixteenth century, who like Gossaert was a follower of Dürer and the first to introduce the Italian Renaissance in the Northern Netherlands. Lucas was an extraordinary painter. He was an infant prodigy. Born in 1494, he had already completed by 1508 engravings and paintings of highest mastership. One of his earliest paintings, which he might have done at the age of fifteen, represents the prophet Daniel as a boy giving witness for Susanna before the judge (Fig. 51; Bremen, Kunsthalle). Lucas' early paintings are distinguished by a harmonious brilliancy of colors, engraving-like perfection, and sharpness of naturalistic and psychological observation. The denseness of the groups causes the figures to rise in Gothic perpendicularity. In his large altar with the Resurrection of the Dead and the Last Judgment, which he painted in 1526, freely moving figures are spread over wide spaces. They reveal a perfect knowledge of the nude, trained through the contact with Dürer and Gossaert, without detriment to the lucidity anl almost plein-airlike lightness of the pictorial texture. Even there, the rhythm of Late Gothic still resounds in flaming curves and jagged silhouettes.

We see how the unity of Late Gothic and Renaissance in the works of the masters of the Netherlands kept alive all the great pictorial achievements of the past. It also preserved the continuance of the visual approach to nature of the old masters in an era which links up the two great centuries of Netherlandish art: the fifteenth and the seventeeth. Diametrically different as they are, Lucas van Leyden's self-portrait in the Museum of Braunschweig, which foreshadows the masterly freedom and liquid brushwork of the paintings by Frans Hals and Rembrandt, and Jan Gossaert's portrait of the children of the King of Denmark in Hampton Court, which gives a foretaste of the vital plasticity of Rubens' portraits, are both landmarks in a historical progress without which the achievements of modern painting would never have been possible.

VI

Soul and Mechanism of the Universe

T HE INFLUENCE of Italian art reshaped Netherlandish painting in the second half of the sixteenth century. The partial
adoption of ancient and Renaissance forms, as we saw it at
the beginning of the century, was replaced by a different organization of the whole composition based on the principles of tectonic
balance, solemn spaciousness, and an enhancement of the figures
which gave them majestic beauty and freedom of movement. The
scientific elements of Renaissance art were completely subordi-
nated to decorative splendor and magnificence of aspect. It was
mainly one event which brought this change about — the influence
of Raphael's classical art, exerted through his large cartoons of the
deeds of Christ and the Apostles which were sent to Brussels as
models for tapestries woven on order of the Vatican. This change
may be clearly noticed in the art of Bernard van Orley, Vrouw
Margaret's court painter. The richly interlaced, exuberant style
of his early works, in line with the Northern tradition, vanishes in
the great rhythms of his tapestries, late works which are of a genuine monumentality. A composition like Abraham Buying the
Burial Place for Sarah's Tomb, from the cycle of scenes of the Old
Testament, is conceived in a Southern spirit.[1] As Roman art was
decisive in the development of this style in the Netherlands, it is
called "Romanism." Romanism in the Netherlands did not keep
this classical Raphaelesque aspect for long. About the middle of
the century it entered a new phase. Composition, which in the era
of Orley had gradually gone over from the Old Netherlandish
tradition into the new classical mode, was completely broken up.
The last vestiges of the Old Netherlandish way of organizing a
picture were swept away. Instead, a profusion of heaving, struggling, conflicting forms appeared. Heemskerck's Entombment of
Christ of 1559–60, in the Museum of Brussels, consists of mighty
figures of heroic stature and type, emphatic and pathetic in every
gesture and movement, in every curve of the bulging lines. The

painter shows his mastery of the human body in an ostentatious way. It is the influence of the heroic style of Michelangelo which has transformed Netherlandish art so radically. The Dutchman Martin van Heemskerck seems to boast of his achievements in the foreign mode which he nevertheless handles in a typically Northern, expressive way. The exaggerated traits in his painting bring to mind the works of the early Antwerp Mannerists. We are reminded of the fact that this whole century in all its artistic productions, from the end of the very short episode of High Renaissance and its classical balance to the beginning of the Baroque, is characterized by features which mean either enhancement and exaltation or scholarly perfection, supreme mastery of anatomy and of the counterpoint of composition. These features are considered as "manneristic." Hence, this whole era of Late Renaissance, which lasted almost one century, is also called the era of "Mannerism." Romanism, the imitation of the colossal Roman style in the Netherlands, is one of its foremost symptoms. All artists traveled to Rome.[2]

Another showpiece of Netherlandish Romanism is the Fall of the Rebellious Angels, painted in 1554 by Frans Floris (Antwerp Museum). Floris was the arch Romanist among the Flemish painters of the middle of the century. Here he seems to have made an attempt to outmatch even Michelangelo's Last Judgment in the ingenious interlacing of nudes to form a great idealistic composition. What distinguishes the works of the Netherlandish imitators of Michelangelo from those of his Italian followers is a considerable amount of purely pictorial qualities in the rendering of substances and the use of colors.

If we turn from Floris' Fall of the Angels to another Flemish picture of the same subject, which was painted eight years later (Fig. 52), we face the strongest and strangest contrast we can imagine. While we still see in Floris' painting a certain equilibrium of above and below, of left and right, the other picture confronts our puzzled eyes with a tumult of fantastic beings, whirling like a snowstorm. At first it is difficult for the onlooker to make out any meaningful shape at all and to find his bearings in this section of the chaos. Soon, however, a high grade of pictorial realization convinces him of the aliveness and meaningfulness of all these monsters. In the painting of Floris we discovered classical Michel-angelesque nudes provided only with monstrous heads, but here we are confronted with the strangest hybrids and offsprings of nightmares. It is hard to enumerate all the categories of devils which the painter has poured out on the panel from the abundance of his imagination. We see birds, fishes, reptiles, lizards, toads, lobsters, oysters, beetles, spiders, butterflies, and all kinds of insects. They appear not only in a tremendous enlargement of their zoomorphic shapes, but also in the most unbelievable blendings with each other, with vegetable and artificial formations. We perceive a flying crawfish with shells for wings, a dragonfly with the body of an artichoke and a poppy head, a bird with a female head, butterfly wings, and a flower's tail. Roasted geese and magpies, flies with bodies inflated to eggs, fishes which tear themselves open like zippers, hurdy-gurdies with lobster heads, infuriated coats of arms savagely fighting, bats which burst into swarms of flies, coral formations blowing trumpets, and insects with Medusa heads alternate with crabs and armors, bears and monkeys. Finally we discover a huge dragon with the heads of the seven-headed monster of the Apocalypse tumbling down in the center; it has the distinction of being killed by St. Michael himself, the leader of the celestial fighters. St. Michael is protected by shiny golden armor, and seems to be carried not only by his huge wings but also by his light blue and moss green mantle which flutters pompously. It cannot be difficult to carry this armed spirit through the air because his long limbs are thin like those of a spider. While the bodies of Floris' angels and demons are solids of an equal natural perfection, the angels are here of the same supernatural structure as the devils. They have been compared with the spectral figures of El Greco, but we may find their counterparts in Gothic art as well. They defeat the demons more through the untouchable serenity of their spirit than through physical strength as in Floris' painting. Their weapons of attack and defense are of a Don Quixote-like ineffectiveness. Only one feature links this painting with its Romanistic contemporaries — a certain generalizing treatment of surfaces, and the delicacy with which colors of high intensity blossom out of warm and cool greys. Everything else is completely different.

As color brings meaning into the turmoil of spirits and demons, so the composition also reveals the cosmic order to which this chaos is subservient. A huge sun in a pale yellow glare, representing the celestial sphere, appears at the upper margin. Out of it pours the stream of demons towards the spectator in rapid, terrifying aggrandizement. The circular curve of this sphere ranges spirits and devils in concentric arches, spreading like the waves of sound in the atmosphere. This movement finds no end at the picture surface. From the bluish grey of the height it spreads into the reddish depth of the inferno at the lower margin and engulfs even the spectator. This event happens in the bottomless space of the universe, the order of which this diabolic shower of meteors cannot disturb; even these freely falling bodies have to obey its laws. An automatic coercion underlies this dynamic whirl of movement. A dashing angel and a giant locust swing as coördinated pendulums from the dim sun. That the position of this sun is eccentric makes the idea of the universe still more gigantic.

The painter of this startling picture in the Museum of Brussels was Pieter Bruegel the Elder, the greatest artist of the Netherlands in the sixteenth century. Only a few documents and a scant biography give information about him, a biography written by the painter Carel van Mander some decades after his death. He died in 1569 after a comparatively short life, and seems to have been born about 1520 in a village of Brabant, as his biographer maintains. He worked in Antwerp where he became master in 1551. From 1561 onward he lived in Brussels, where he married the daughter of his former master Pieter Coecke van Alost. Van Mander adds that one hardly could look at any of his pictures without laughing, or at least smiling; that he worked in the manner of Hieronymus Bosch, and therefore was called Pieter the jester. He liked to mix with peasants at weddings and kermesses in their native costume, and to frighten friends and pupils with diabolic hoaxes. As for the rest,. he was a quiet and contemplative man.

This is not too much to know about so great an artist, although it is more than we know about Hieronymus Bosch. Bosch was already dead when Bruegel was born — there is an interval of three generations between them. His works prove that van Mander was right in saying that Bruegel worked occasionally in the manner of Bosch, although he was far from imitating him. The wings of Bosch's moralizing triptychs like The Garden of Pleasures and The Hay-Waggon reveal the sources of Bruegel's inspiration. There we see a similar tumult of diabolic monsters; celestial and human beings are of a similar attenuation and spiritualization. There, for the first time, we see the demons leave the celestial region like a stream of locusts. Bruegel harked back; he revived an art of the past, an art which belonged to the Middle Ages. Bosch himself stood aloof from the naturalistic problems of his contemporaries, and looked back to the refined and spiritualized art of 1400.[3] With Bruegel begins a historical revival of the Middle Ages which increased toward the dawn of the Baroque, a revival to which the historical dramas of Shakespeare belong as much as the drawings and engravings by Netherlandish artists in Late Gothic style. The group of the mourning Marys in Bruegel's Carrying of the Cross in Vienna reminds us of the paintings by the Master of Flémalle and of the statuary grandeur of medieval sculptures. Bruegel even increased the attenuation of supernatural figures beyond Bosch and stylized them according to a medieval canon. He distinguished them from earthly proportions which look twice as massive beside them. We see this in the Parable of the Wise and Foolish Virgins [4] where the freed souls and the angels compete with the Gothic architecture in flamboyant elevation while the Virgins' earthly life rolls off in a realism comparable to Shakespeare's popular scenes. It rotates in bulky circles: at the right, the round-dance of the Foolish Virgins; at the left, the pious work of the Wise Virgins, bent over the mighty rounds of reel, tub, and basket. In Bosch's works heaven and earth fuse in one magic, unreal world. Here, they are distinguished. In Bosch's panels, the groups are scattered in a whimsical fashion. Here, they are concentrated in monumental accents. The circular rhythm goes through everything. It is similar to the cosmic organization of the battle of the angels. Heaven and earth, in spite of their discrimination, are comprehended in one great mechanism which functions with automatic regularity.

When Christ enters Limbo,[5] he is enclosed in a sphere of light with an angels' orchestra which rolls and floats through gorges between tremendous masks like a soap bubble. We could compare this with a diving bell as well which protects the Lord in the thick air of Hell through which a fish swims with a brood of ravens in a basket, a Gothic helmet propels itself, and a mill wheel revolves slowly driven by poor souls instead of water. The hellish cosmos, too, works like a huge clockwork in which many cogwheels interlock, although disorder threatens now and the devils take defensive measures in haste.

Bruegel made a considerable amount of drawings of this kind.[6] They are not projects for paintings, but models for engravers. The publisher Hieronymus Cock in Antwerp was Bruegel's patron, who had his drawings of moral, didactic, or scenic content reproduced in engravings and scattered in countless impressions over the country. This was the time of the tremendous rise of reproductive engraving and instructive literature which began to spread erudition and education throughout all classes.

The contrast of Bruegel's art to his surroundings has been a great puzzle to art historians. Bruegel seemed to be so isolated in his time that the question arose as to the origins of his art. Some scholars have considered him as the restorer of a national Netherlandish art who opposed the imported international Romanism, a symbol of the foreign Spanish rule in the country, by elevating the native peasantry and folklore.[7] This seemed to be proved not only by Carel van Mander's report but also by many sketchbook drawings which Bruegel apparently did on his trips in the country, careful notations of what he saw. He drew for instance a Team of Cart Horses, plump and simple-minded creatures like their master.[8] Bruegel carefully inscribed the variegated colors in order to remember them when he created figures of that kind on his panels. But Bruegel had been in Rome, and although he reacted to the South in a way different from the other Flemings, there is no doubt that it made a deep and lasting impression on him. His relation to the spirit of Italian art and scenery was a much deeper and more essential one than that of the Romanists, who remained on the surface. In 1568, one year before his death, he made a vigorous drawing of the Harvesters in Hamburg where the monumental figure of a drinking peasant sprawls in the foreground; it was taken from a Michelangelesque nude and adapted to the Flemish subject. Bruegel knew well to use Italian achievements for the great, rolling, synthesized forms of his late style.

Opposing the theory of a rustic and national Flemish art as a protest against a foreign mode, other scholars have stressed the point that Bruegel's art was not at all created for peasants but was an art for educated connoisseurs of the upper classes. Indeed, Bruegel never painted works for churches or public places; his paintings hung in the houses of collectors. Only the engravings were destined for the broad masses. The particular style of his paintings was assumed to be rooted in the courtly fashion of water-color paintings on canvas with profane subjects, which were much favored in aristocratic circles beginning with the late Middle Ages.[9] There are preserved water-color paintings of this kind from the end of Bruegel's career, as for instance The Pessimist in Naples who wears mourning because of the wickedness of the World which furtively deprives him of his purse. Yet we do not know of such works from the early years. No documented works before his journey to Italy in 1552/53 are preserved. So the theory that Bruegel's art arose from an unnoticed by-current of Netherlandish art which kept alive the fifteenth-century naturalism does not find much confirmation in his works either.[10] Even if we felt inclined to consider Patenier's "world landscapes" as such a by-current, Bruegel's grasp of the cosmic totality is so different from those fancy rockeries, that a clandestine Northern tradition cannot offer a satisfactory explanation. No Late Gothic tradition can explain the symphonic grandeur of the Fortified City of 1553 (drawing in the British Museum), growing out of earth and rock under a somber sky, swarming with the life of men, animals, and plants. The feeling of such an extremely modern landscape is nearer to Titian than to any Old Flemish tradition.

This seems to limit the Old Netherlandish, the Gothicizing tendency in Bruegel's work to a group of figure compositions. There is no doubt that it dominates the illustration of the proverb The Large Fishes Eat the Little Ones (Fig. 54).[11] A large perch is stranded. Little men deal with it; one opens its belly with a tremendous knife which is marked with the astronomical sign of the "Earth" as an indication that this is the way of earthly affairs. There is none so small that he would not swallow a still smaller one. Two human legs grow out of the body of one of the fishes; with a smaller fish in his mouth, he passes by a tree on which other small fishes already hang. The little scoundrels are hung while the large ones escape. This is human life, mirrored in a proverb. Proverbs contain old popular wisdom. They play a great part in all satirical art and literature of the Late Middle Ages, in the writings of Sebastian Brant, Murner, and Gailer von Keisersperg as much as in the paintings of Bosch. Bruegel's connection with them in the contents of his pictures has been observed repeatedly.[12] When this drawing was engraved, Hieronymus Bosch was indicated as the inventor, not Bruegel. Possibly Bruegel took the idea from Bosch, whose inventions, too, were published by Cock in print. Yet Bruegel certainly transformed the idea completely in his own imagination.

As Bruegel harks back to the old moralists and satirists, a further theory for the archaic, historizing features in his art has been produced: Bruegel was a painting philosopher, a sceptic and ironic pessimist, a Platonist and Stoic, therefore, he adopted in his work the style of the old satirists.[13] To this theory the objection may be raised that Bruegel also used this medieval style in works which definitely have no satirical meaning. The solemnity and monumentality of the Adoration of the Magi (1564) in London conjures up the great spirit and the inward quality of a composition by Hugo van der Goes. St. Joseph and the man who whispers into his ear are derived from an engraving by Schongauer.[14] We see the group of the Marys in the Carrying of the Cross filled with the ecclesiastic austerity of the works of the Master of Flémalle.

A similar medieval rigidity can be observed in the drawing of the Albertina, Painter and Connoisseur (Fig. 53). Both men wear medieval costumes which enhance the monumentality of the composition in half-lengths. De Tolnay regarded the drawing as an ironical self-portrait of Bruegel. Certainly, the master intended to contrast the painter's state of ruggedness and poverty with the smoothness and vanity of the well-dressed enthusiast. The fanaticism, the inward wrath of the creative artist who, forgetting the world around him, has to follow his inner urge and complete his work even at the cost of hardship of life, and the complacency of the dilettante are made clear in an unmistakable way. But it is

not without significance that the costumes are medieval and not
contemporary. Thus Bruegel could also have intended to show
persons of a past time. I would not exclude entirely the possibility
that Bruegel meant to characterize in this way his great model
Bosch, the man living in his own strange world outside of time,
although in this case the portrait would be only an ideal one and
not accord with the real features of Bosch. The admiration of the
connoisseur is as sincere as the creative furor of the artist, and expressed by the thrust of his hand into his purse showing the eagerness to acquire a fine work of art. Bruegel had a friend of this kind,
too, the merchant Franckert who accompanied him on his excur-
sions. The connoisseur's face becomes almost blank from wonder-
ment, a startled mask in which the mouth opens like a cut with
a knife.

In using the word "mask," we hit upon a point which is essential for the understanding of Bruegel's art. Bruegel avoids detailed
and descriptive psychology in faces. His figures wish to keep their
anonymity, their exclusive value as general human beings. They
seem to hide something before us. They like to turn their backs
upon us, to disregard us, like the audience in the Sermon of St.
John in the Museum of Budapest (1566). This is very different
from the show put up by the Romanists. Gypsies and Indians,
mendicant friars and burghers, pilgrims and Turks alike exhibit
their broad backs, hats and caps. The salmon pink, lemon yellow,
grey, red, white, and earth brown clothes are rendered with an
amazing feeling of material, superior to any Old Netherlandish
master. Bruegel was a magician with the brush. Yet his persons
do not reveal *what* they feel and think, although they feel and
think *very strongly*. In the background, where they stare up at
the preacher, the faces become light disks in which the dark holes
of the eyes and mouths gape, puzzling and strange. They seem to
have more hold on the speaker than the speaker has on them. The
disklike character is applied to everything — to details as well as to
silhouettes. This is still more surprising in the face of the amazing,
microscopic substantiality which breathes in barky trees, plants,
and muddy ground of the forest. Yet through this disklike character Bruegel expresses all the more intensely the enigmatic inner
life of his beings in all its unpredictability and inscrutability. *This*

seems to me one of the main reasons why Bruegel harked back to the simplified medieval forms. On Burgundian tombs of 1400 we see the so-called "pleureurs," mourners, so much enveloped in their cowls that they disappear in complete anonymity. Bruegel created similar figures in a magnificent late proverb drawing in the Print Room at Berlin, which represents beekeepers at their work. Of course, he saw them in reality. But it is significant that he chose a subject where man vanishes into an animated, blocklike anonymity.

What is the meaning of this anonymity of man in Bruegel's works? This notion of man is not isolated; it also occurs in the contemporary philosophical thought. Bruegel was an intellectual at the height of his time, as we know from the fundamental research of Max Dvořák.[15] He was in contact with leading spirits, among whom the religious philosopher Coornhert, the publisher Plantin, and the geographer Ortelius deserve special mention. Ideas as they moved the thought and science of his time found expression in his work, too.[16] Bruegel apparently was one of those men of reflective and contemplative temper who stood aloof from the great bustle and made up their minds about it. Another was Sebastian Franck, who had died before Bruegel began his work, yet remarkably agrees with him in some aspects of world and mankind, as Charles de Tolnay rightly observed. Franck gave the following definition of mankind: "Vita una et eadem omnibus. There is one equal life on earth. Omnis homo unus homo. All men one man. Who sees one natural man, sees them all." [17] At these words, we see the disklike and masklike faces of Bruegel's figures gaze at us. Man is understood as anonymous mass, subservient to the great laws which rule all events on earth, as they rule the circuits of the globes in the universe. *One great mechanism is the content of the universe.* Daily life, the sorrows and pleasures of man, unroll as it is precalculated in this clock-work.

In his early paintings, Bruegel chooses a high standpoint so that he looks upon the stage of human life as if from a watchtower, also in a metaphorical sense. From it he observes the swarming life of these human ants. These paintings in all their vigorous, startling and amusing portrayal of holiday and everyday, become symbolical of the whole human race. When Ash Wednesday approached, a combat between Carnival and Lent was staged on the squares of the old Flemish towns.[18] Bruegel in 1559 gave a picture of such an old community with the little gable houses in deep violet and brown brickwork underneath green roofs (Fig. 55; Vienna, Kunsthistorisches Museum). They frame the square thoughtfully, darkening in the moist air of approaching spring. Life swarms out of them, checkered and variegated. Windows are cleaned, waffles baked, fishes sold. On the left, Carnival and its gaiety comes to an end. On the right, out of the church full of the earnestness of Lent with veiled images, pour devotees in black cloaks. People think of charity again. At the head of the procession haggard Lent is pulled by a monk and a nun into the battle against fat Carnival who is shoved on a barrel against his adversary. Children have their fun on both sides, to the left with maskers and waffles, to the right with pretzels and rattles. The whole revolves in a huge circle in which many small wheels pleasantly whirl.

The panel of the Children's Plays of 1560 is based on the same principle. It contains hundreds of plays and games, most of them still alive today. Children in their games were considered as a likeness of the queerness of the adult, and so this painting, too, has a moral meaning.[19] The conceited walk on stilts; others look at the world upside down. The whole mass of children whirls and turns in countless little circles and dies away in the hazy distance of the perspective of the street. Round and rolling also are the forms of the single groups and figures.

The painting of the Flemish Proverbs of 1559 in Berlin contains an encyclopedia of all human wisdom under the fool's cap. We could interpret it for hours; books have been written on it.[20] The performance takes place in the inn at the sign of the world turned upside down and nearby. A crowd of people are most assiduously occupied with the queerest activities, literal representations of the countless metaphors through which popular wit expresses the vanity and folly of so many human enterprises. We see the man who throws roses before pigs; the peasant who fills up with earth the fountain after the calf has been drowned; the woman who hangs a blue cloak over her husband (makes him a cuckold). The braggart makes the world dance on his thumb, and the hypocrite succeeds in tying a flaxen beard even around the face of our Lord.

"Much screaming for little wool" says another and shears a pig. The man who butts his head against a wall is present as well as the one who ties a bell around the neck of the cat. Another takes great pains in carrying light in a basket from the illuminated inn into the bright day. In the attic, fools are shaved, and a man shoots one arrow after the other, to illustrate superfluous efforts. Pancakes grow on the roof, and a nagging old woman is so horribly persistent that she succeeds in tying down the devil on a pillow. It is the proverb type of the "Dulle Griet" (crazy Margaret), the Flemish Xantippe who undertakes a warlike expedition into hell where she makes rich booty of treasures and kitchen utensils. The devils are terribly upset about the invasion of the crazy Margarets, and try to protect themselves with the most unusual means of defense. In 1562, Bruegel depicted this in a wonderful panel (Musée Mayer van den Bergh, Antwerp) where the whole sky glows in the red of the conflagration.

If we ask where in the literature of the sixteenth century a similar grasp of the totality of life, of nature and the cosmos can be observed, we have to mention Rabelais and Shakespeare. In the fifth book of his novel *Pantagruel*, which appeared in 1562, Rabelais describes how his hero arrives at the court of Quintessence, the Queen of Whims, and inspects her country Entelechy. There, we get a glimpse of a fool's paradise as Bruegel painted it. Gargantua sees the Queen's officers who wash moors white, plow the sandy beach with yokes of foxes, shear asses to get long fleecy wool, and do many other useful things. The proverb uses metaphors. Bruegel represents them literally, and thus achieves his comical effects. In the same way, the characters of Shakespeare's comedies take puns and metaphors literally in order to obtain the absurd results which make the audience laugh.

All these swarming people are represented in the same picture-sheet style, in gay, unbroken, lucid colors. They look naïve, awkward, and disklike, and remind us of the figures in a fifteenth-century print. At the same time, they have the character of automatons which gaily whiz round in the mechanism of the world. *It is the idea of the mechanism of the universe*, which in the later sixteenth century also dominated the systems of the philosophers Bernardino Telesio, Tommaso Campanella, and Giordano Bruno, of the astronomers and geographers. The creator once established this mechanism, but now it goes its own lawful way. It is the task of the perspicuous brains to demonstrate its laws in writing and painting. The church and its theological metaphysics can no longer interfere with it. The era of a new rational understanding of the world approaches. Bruegel's friend, the geographer Ortelius,[21] in his atlas Theatrum Orbis Terrarum made the first attempt to give a faithful picture of the totality of our globe. The same cosmographic concept underlies the grandiose mastery of space in Bruegel's View of the Harbour of Naples (Rome, Galleria Doria), his oldest painting of which we know, done shortly after his return from Italy. The idea of the round, of the circle dominates the landscape as much as the figure paintings, and transmits the feeling of the huge vault of the globe to the spectator. We find the same kind of cosmic landscape in another early painting; The Fall of Icarus (Fig. 56; Brussels, Museum). It is a remarkable proof of Bruegel's attitude towards classical antiquity,[22] because it illustrates the version of the story which Ovid gave in his Metamorphoses. Ploughman, shepherd, and angler are taken from the Latin text, yet while they observe the catastrophe with anxiety in Ovid's verses, they quietly attend to their work in Bruegel's picture, without taking notice of the unfortunate aviator whose legs are just disappearing in the waves of the sea.[23] Nature takes its great, lawful course, undisturbed by a single human fate. The yellow sun sets in the West. The sea, the coasts, and islands, spreading like a map over the terrestrial dome, shimmer in silvery hues. A haze of light fills the universe and transfigures the scenery.[24]

As earth and the celestial globes obey the laws of the universe, so the human race obeys laws which anthropology and social sciences tried to discover in the coming centuries. Bruegel, even before these sciences accepted their modern shape, gave a pictorial forecast of their concept of a lawfully regulated totality. Hence the mechanical clockwork appearance of his cosmography of the human race, the anonymous, automaton-like character of his figures. What style of figure representation would have better fitted this general, anonymous, automaton-like world than the stiff, thin-limbed, disklike, archaic figure style of the painters of the late Middle Ages? *This is the main reason why Bruegel harked back to Hieronymus Bosch and the mode of the fifteenth century.*

Nothing can be compared with the oppressive grandeur and

stirring actuality with which the medieval world is conjured up in the tremendous Triumph of Death (Madrid, Prado). A gloomy era began in the Netherlands. The reaction of the Spanish rulers suppressed the religious and national liberty of spirit in the open-minded Netherlands. The eighty years' war was impending. Bruegel's intellectual friends were in danger of their lives. The autos-da-fé of the Inquisition reddened the sky as in this sinister picture. It is the old Gothic Dance of Death, multiplied to symphonic grandeur. Holbein in his famous woodcut series gave classical significance in the sense of the High Renaissance to single groups. Bruegel conjured up the polyphony of the Middle Ages but endowed it with a modern meaning — a process significant for the time of Late Renaissance or Mannerism. A savage fight between the dead and the living goes on in the foreground, yet the outcome is not in doubt. There are too many reserves of dead, waiting behind coffin lids which they use as shields. And finally, all living beings are driven into a huge coffin which opens like a mouse trap.

How far remote from medieval art these mass scenes actually are is proved by the representations of the Seven Virtues in a cycle of drawings. They belonged to the standard repertory of late medieval art, frequently represented in book illuminations.[25] The allegorical females play a very small part in Bruegel's drawings where the autonomous mechanism of human society with all its devices rolls off. In the representation of Justice (Brussels, Royal Library) real and fictitious crimes automatically find their punishment. So the most cruel methods of torture and execution, which will hardly cure the perversion of the world, are displayed.

I have emphasized so much the mechanism of the universe in Bruegel's art that the question could arise whether his concept considers the existent world as something entirely mechanical and materialistic, void of soul and mood. To answer this question, let us turn to Bruegel's landscapes. Quite a group of drawings from the years of his Italian journey are preserved. They do not show ancient ruins, the grandeur of Old Rome, like the drawings of the Romanists, but idyllic pictures of the Italy of his time — a river embankment, a monastery among blossoming trees, and above all the grandeur of the Alps which he crossed on his way to the South.

This experience struck him as it had struck Dürer. But it made a more lasting impression on him — it remained rooted in him almost until the end of his life. Van Mander wrote, "It was said of him, that while he visited the Alps, he had swallowed all the mountains and cliffs, and, upon coming home, he had spit them forth upon his canvases and panels." Saul on his way to Damascus is struck down by the celestial ray in a mountain notch (Vienna, 1567). The Dolomite towers, cut by the picture frame like the rising conical shapes of the larch firs, extend into the infinite. Floating layers of clouds girdle them. We guess the presence of the celestial sphere only from a tremendous amphitheater of clouds. We feel almost dizzy if we look down into the depth of the gorge through which the soldiers climb up, slowly and with pain. Only an artist who had seen this in reality could have painted it so convincingly. Bruegel has rendered the character and spirit of this scenery in an incomparable way. The huge mass of a rocky mountain range rises before our eyes in a drawing (Fogg Museum of Art) where we walk down to a village situated between trees.[26] The onlooker himself believes he moves in the scenery, so suggestive is Bruegel's interpretation of it. Bruegel not only rendered the cartographic shape of the mountains but also the cosmic life which dwells in them, which makes them grow and decay. They are like animated beings, endowed with character. The down of the forests sprouts on them; everywhere the organic life of nature is astir. The dotting touch of the pen lends color and vibrancy to the drawing, and at the same time evokes the impression of a procreative aboriginal substance. In just the same way, the surface of Bruegel's landscape paintings is alive.

The largest collection of Bruegel's paintings is preserved in the Kunsthistorisches Museum in Vienna, owing to the patronage of Emperor Rudolph II who was an admirer of Bruegel's art. There can be found a quite unique series of landscape paintings by the master. Even the holy events of the Gospel are interwoven with the eternal revolution of nature. A spring landscape full of moisture and freshness offers the setting for the Carrying of the Cross (1564). Rain had drenched the country so that the procession has to wade through mud holes. A low ceiling of rain clouds still hovers in the distance at the right where the mass crowds in a large circle around the place of execution. The weather clears up at the left. The city of Jerusalem appears in a light, opalizing morning mist, and the sun breaks through victoriously. Everyone hurries, on horseback and by foot, not to miss anything of the thrilling performance. The central group is almost submerged by the life of the mass.

A companion piece to this picture forms the Census of the People at Bethlehem on Christmas Eve (1566) in the Museum of Brussels (Fig. 57), illustrating the narrative of the second book of the Gospel of St. Luke. It is a wonderful idyll of a Flemish village deeply covered with snow, full of the homely activity of peasants and burghers on the eve of a great holiday. Before the inn at the sign of the green wreath, they slaughter pigs and upholster chairs. Barrels with fresh beer have arrived. The census officers have put up their office in the inn; the census is combined with tax payment. People already queue up at the window. St. Joseph is just arriving with the Virgin, but they do not attract our attention at all among the crowd. People gather from all sides. Children skate, slide, and throw snowballs. The Bible illustration becomes a perfect realistic genre picture of the painter's own time — a fact of tremendous importance for the future. *Life itself* in all its various forms is presented as the main content, just as later in Shakespeare's Henry IV the main action is woven into manifold genre scenes. Here, the painter took hold not only of the mood of nature, of the homely old village buried in the spell of winter, but also of the mood of men. The mass of people, although it moves coercively, is not void of soul, but one great animated being, like nature.

The *soul* of nature also speaks to us in the epical grandeur of the painted cycle of the months completed in 1565.[27] The idea of such a cycle goes back to the calendars of the Gothic Books of Hours where each month was provided with an appropriate illustration of the aspect offered by nature in it, and of the seasonal human activities. In the same year, Bruegel began a cycle of drawings representing the seasons to which the Harvesters of 1568 mentioned before belongs. Spring (in the Albertina, 1565) represents gardening in one of the geometrically laid out gardens which were fashionable in the era of Mannerism. In his panel series, Bruegel shows the great, freely growing open nature. A winter month,

December or January, gives a prospect of the wide country with plains, seacoasts and mountains, seen from a hill. Nature is held in chains by the spell of cold. The only source of light is the surfaces radiant with snow. The motionless sky darkens in deep greenish grey. Hunters with a pack of freezing dogs step down the hill. The figures appear as dark silhouettes in the shining white. But nature only slumbers. Life is astir everywhere. Skaters and sliders wheel round on the frozen ponds, carriages move over the highways, and smoke rises from the snow-covered huts. We can find pictures of ravishing beauty within Bruegel's pictures.

The Gloomy Day is the name of a painting which represents February or March. It is filled with the melancholy mood of thaw and early spring. People are beginning to cut the trees. The south wind roars through the black branches and stirs up the waves of the sea so that they wreck the ships. The dark earth begins to breathe; its saps rise again; the village is huddled up in its shadow. The deep brown, full of a hidden glow, seems to be pregnant with the forces of new growth. Most startling is the snow-covered chain of high mountains with glaciers in a weird bluish light, like moonlight, which filters through layers of clouds. Only Leonardo da Vinci and Altdorfer expressed the ghostlike majesty of high mountains with an equal mastery.

The only original etching created by Bruegel, the Rabbit Hunt (1566), seems to repeat the composition of one of the lost spring months of the series. Nature flourishes in the tender down of spring. The trees are resplendent in the light garb of their first leaves. Again, colorful vibrancy is achieved by a dotting method of drawing which is a characteristic of Bruegel, and can also be noticed in the brushwork of his paintings. The pictorial structure of his pictures is utterly alive and diaphanous, in spite of its perfection. The surface of the landscapes almost seems to be the germinating and growing of nature itself instead of its pictorial transcription. It lies like a down, a hue, a veil of mycoderm over the glazes, conjuring up mosses in the foreground and high forests in the distance. In the rendering of nature Bruegel achieved an animism and sensualism which Campanella tried to establish philosophically in his book "On the Senses of Things and Magic." [28] Campanella endows everything in nature with senses, not only humans and animals, but the whole cosmos. "Heaven and earth and the world *feel*, like the smallest microbes."

The oneness of life often brings its different emanations so near to each other that they blend. The picture of June (Raudnitz, Collection of Prince Lobkowitz) shows the harvesters carrying fruit baskets under which their heads almost disappear. It looks as if the humans were shooting up into fruits and flowers.

The picture of July or August in the Metropolitan Museum of Art is the only documented work by Bruegel in the United States. The golden glare of the grain floods over the rolling country. The peasants hold their midday rest beneath a tree; a farm-laborer comes up with water jugs through a path cut in the grain. A haze of brooding summer heat hovers over the earth.

The maturest and grandest of these pictures of the months is the November in Vienna (Fig. 58). Winter approaches. The peasants drive the cattle from the alpine pastures to the villages. The cows, looking like toys, stamp through a mixture of mud and fallen leaves. The rusty color symphony of Fall spreads over the country. Vintagers still work in the vineyards. The air feels cool, shimmering in a light blue under the clear sky at the left, darkening in a deep greenish blue under the stripes of rain clouds approaching from the right. The composition has the cosmic openness of the early world landscapes, yet a monumentality in which the impression made by the works of the Venetian masters for the first time seems to have fully matured. Its nearness to nature is unmatched in the history of art. The distance becomes lucid and fluid in the air saturated with moisture so that we can distinguish every little house, chapel, and tree on the opposite slope of the valley.

There is no other artist who could have surpassed Bruegel in this amazing grasp of the soul of nature. Cosmos and universe were to him, indeed, not only a mechanism but also a great animated being. Bruegel in his paintings and drawings has definitely conquered the idea of the universe as an infinite which has form and shape subservient to great cosmic laws. The picture of the Sea Storm (Vienna), illustrating the parable of the whale who plays around with an empty barrel and forgets to swallow the ship, is just such an embracing of the vastness of the globe, water-covered, blackish brown and green, illuminated by an unwhole-some light. In the philosophy of the Late Renaissance we find the grandeur of the ordered infinite expressed by Giordano Bruno in his "Dialogues on the Infinite, Universe and Worlds." [29] He was the first scientific thinker who considered the universe not as something limited like the Ptolemaic system of spheres, but as the continuous and unlimited ethereal space in which countless celestial globes follow their courses. The mechanism of the universe consists of their circuits. *Yet every single celestial body moves by its own impulse, because it is animated by its own soul. Their countless totality forms the soul of the universe.*

The proud attitude of the creative man toward this universe is that of a positive and heroic independence. "The captain of all impulses and thoughts is the human will who stands on the stern of the ship of his life; with the oar of reason he steers the inner impulses and feelings through all waves of outer accidents." [30] It is a feeling of life which Bruegel documented in his engraved series of proud naval vessels (Bastelaer, nos. 98–108).

Man such as he is, in all the grandeur of life, without classical idealization, is the content of Bruegel's last paintings. They gained the admiration of Rubens who tried to continue their great and monumental vein in his peasant paintings. The Parable of the Blind Men who drag each other into the ditch (Naples, 1568) illustrates more strikingly than anything else the inexorability of fate impending over the humans who grope and tumble in dark-ness. Nothing can be compared to the tragic expression of these faces staring like masks with empty eye sockets into the clear light of the day which they cannot see.

The Proverb of the Bird's Nest (Vienna) places the single figure of a peasant, growing mightily out of space like one of Michel-angelo's heroes, in a Flemish landscape picture of such an intimacy and grandeur that no less than the amplitude of the universe is present in this small section of it. Here, Bruegel anticipates the essence of Dutch landscape art of the seventeenth century, just as he created in the Sea Storm the first marine painting, a type so much in favor with seventeenth-century Dutchmen.

The figures of the Peasant Wedding (Vienna), where the cooks serve the dishes on a barn door taken from its hinges, have the unerring firmness of spheres moving in their circuits, while at the same time they are full of soul and overflowing vigor.

The rustic dancers and carousers of the Kermess (Vienna) are of earthly weightiness, yet they seem to move on the wings of a cosmic gayness. There is no longer any need of a panoramic view of little automatons in medieval stiffness, because man walks as his own monument on the earth which he enjoys. What the Romanists strove for in vain here finds its natural fulfillment.

VII

The Ancient and the Gothic Revival in French Art and Literature

THE COUNTRY which had taken the lead in the art and culture of the Middle Ages, France, did not play so prominent a role about 1500 as did Italy, Germany, and the Netherlands. It almost looks as if France, which had spent her force throughout the centuries in an uninterrupted stream, slackened at the end of the fifteenth century, when in the neighboring countries a concentration of the creative forces occurred. France was filled with that refined languishing echo of the Middle Ages which the French themselves call *détente*, and which found its best expression in some works of sculpture. A poetic tenderness is perhaps the foremost quality of the works of the *détente*. This was to become of great importance for the future. After a brief fallow period, the sixteenth century brought forth a new crop in which poetry had no inconsiderable share. The fine arts were not impaired as they were in Germany by Reformation problems, but they had to share their prominence with literature. And it was mainly in literature that the French made their great national contribution to the sixteenth century. Therefore, a joint consideration will prove helpful for the understanding of both.

The movement was more closely linked with the cultural program of the rulers than in any other country. It was not the individual struggle of artists and scholars alone, as in Germany and the Netherlands, which brought about the discussion of the new achievements of the Italian Renaissance. It was more the planned activity of the sovereigns which opened new possibilities to artists and writers. French culture in the sixteenth century was not a culture of burghers as in Germany and the Netherlands, but a court culture — and thus far, a continuation of the medieval order. King Francis I's patronage of the fine arts gave a decisive turn to the whole development. His sister Marguerite of Navarre fostered humanism and literature. Henry II reaped the fruits of what his predecessors had planted.

If we consider the revival of classical antiquity as a significant feature of the new Renaissance culture, France was in retard compared with the other countries. The climax of this revival was reached in France about the middle of the sixteenth century, when it had passed the summit elsewhere. *It is embodied in the arts by the School of Fontainebleau; in literature by the poets of the Pléiade.* Although the greater importance rests with the poets, the painters have the priority in time and were of the greatest influence on the development of the poetical imagery. In order to understand the situation at the time of Henry II, we have to study the foundations laid by Francis and Marguerite in the first half of the century.

Francis I considered himself a connoisseur of painting, and he had the enthusiasm of a great collector. He saw his artistic ideal in the Italian Renaissance. When he was a young man, his expeditions and travels brought him in close contact with its sources. His agents in Italy tried to procure as many works of art as they could in order to transfer them to France. Francis even tried to transplant the masters themselves. Leonardo da Vinci spent the last years of his life in Cloux. Andrea del Sarto was in the service of the monarch for one year. A systematic colonization of France by Italian artists began after 1528, when the king rebuilt the old castle in the idyllic surroundings of the forests and ponds of Fontainebleau. It was his favorite place; going to Fontainebleau he called "going home." The king succeeded in making Fontainebleau a concrete symbol of the new fashion. It was praised as a "new Rome" by Vasari, the authoritative Italian critic of the sixteenth century. This success was due to the large-scale activity of Italian masters in Fontainebleau.[1] They settled in the country, permeated it with a new artistic gospel, and at the same time assimilated themselves to its tradition. Thus, an artistic culture of quite unique flavor arose, based on Italian Renaissance in form, on Latinism and Graecism in literary content, and on the French heritage in spirit.

Marguerite of Navarre, a noble and liberally minded character, was open to all progressive thought in the humanities and literature.

She was one of the most educated women of her time. She studied not only the modern but also the ancient languages. Despériers translated Plato's dialogue "Lysis" for her. She favored Clément Marot as a poet. But she was also, with all the mystic and loving fervor of her soul, a protector of religious reformers like Calvin. She left a considerable literary work, best known among it the *Heptameron* which follows the novels of Boccaccio. With her began the enthusiasm for the simple, unspoiled charm of nature, for the bucolic, which was to play such an important part in the poetry of the Pléiade.

Florentine painting had a considerable influence on the royal taste. Contact with Leonardo and Andrea educated Francis in the appreciation of Florentine art. The first phase of the School of Fontainebleau was in the Florentine tradition. In 1531, Giovanni Battista Rosso, called Il Rosso Fiorentino,[2] arrived at Fontainebleau and became the undisputed leader of the artistic enterprises there. Rosso's art was under the dual influence of Michelangelo and Andrea del Sarto. He developed from the mode of his models a highly expressive, almost exaggerated style with elongated figures, harsh contrasts, acute angles, opposing all harmonious roundness and balance. His compositions like the Deposition from the Cross in Volterra, 1521, reveal a tendency toward the transcendental and superhuman. They rise in Gothic steepness and clearly work out the medieval tendencies in the art of Michelangelo. We notice the same tendency in the art of an artist of the same age, Pontormo, whose compositions rise flamingly and longingly toward heaven. With Pontormo and Rosso begins what we call Mannerism in Italian art.[3] We emphasized in the last chapter that Mannerism was more than a particular group or fraction of the general development.[4] The art of the Mannerists in the North and South clearly developed features which were valid in various transformations for almost a century. So in the history of art it is customary to call the long era of Late Renaissance which follows the very short, almost episodelike, era of High Renaissance also the era of "Mannerism." Mannerism lasted from the 1520's until the beginning of the seventeenth century.

As French art of the sixteenth century kept alive underground the tendencies of Gothic, it was a matter of course that Rosso's art would appeal to the French taste. The Italian influence on French art in the sixteenth century was a predominantly manneristic one. The first work which was begun in the castle was the Gallery of Francis I, a long corridor adorned with frescoes which are framed by a profuse decoration in wood and stucco, carvings and mouldings. The impression is that of splendor and magnificence, and at the same time of a fantastic crowding which lends to the Southern forms something of the unsurveyable, entangled aspect of Northern sculpture of the Late Middle Ages. Rosso certainly was responsible for the whole design, of which the figure composition forms only a part. Dispersed among the architectonic elements are nudes in contorted counterpoises, struggling in the narrow space allotted to them. They are seemingly inspired by Michelangelo's Sistine ceiling and the allegorical figures of the Medici tombs. The subjects of the murals are taken from classical mythology, history, and poetry. Homer's *Iliad* and *Odyssey*, Herodotus' and Valerius Maximus' writings, Apuleius' *Amor and Psyche*, and Ovid's *Metamorphoses* are the literary sources. The compositions, like the Death of Adonis, are developed in sharp splintery forms which also lend to the nudes a decorative and unreal appearance. It is the same quality which we see in Rosso's cool and clear-colored easel paintings. As the frescoes have suffered rather much through later overpainting, we may use the original drawings as a help in reconstructing the genuine rhythm of these works. Many of them have survived. The Instruction of Achilles (Paris, École des Beaux-Arts) by the Centaur Chiron in fighting, riding, and swimming proves the master's great ability to concentrate an agitated composition in a limited field to a graceful pattern. Pictorial qualities are far from this art; most of its effect rests with the eloquence of line. Therefore, these delicate preparatory drawings give a perfect idea of the artistic aim striven for. The Mannerists were outstanding draughtsmen. We may also gain an idea of the original splendor of this work from another source. I have already mentioned the importance of the art of tapestry to the Northern countries. A set of tapestries in the Museum of Vienna [5] reproduces the various sections of the Gallery of Francis I. It is marvelous how the harmonious richness of these creations, full of a subdued luster and sparkle of gold, transfers the heavy contrasts of architecture, sculpture, and paint into the dreamlike, imaginary realm of the Gobelin — an enhanced poetry such as was the final aim of this art (Fig. 59).

The poetical quality of the inventions increases. A garden house, the Pavilion of Pomona, was adorned with fresco cycles by the Italian masters. The story of Vertumnus and Pomona taken from Ovid was illustrated by Rosso. The building no longer exists, but Rosso's delicate designs give an excellent idea of the fanciful and whimsical work.[6] Vertumnus, the God of Autumn, in the disguise of an old woman, ardently tries to persuade Pomona, the Goddess of the fruitbearing trees, who ponders over his proposals with a naïve and girlish gesture (Fig. 60). A female genius with butterfly wings and several amoretti who take the beauty under a cross fire of their arrows are grouped near. A fence, a garden door, a pond, and maskerons with fruit garlands complete the setting of a bucolic and courtly stage on which the scene takes place. The poetical imagination creates an atmosphere in which a fancied past and contemporary fashion blend.

One of the most beautiful illustrations of the legend of Vertumnus and Pomona is a series of tapestries woven after designs of the Flemish artist J. C. Vermeyen in the style of Fontainebleau, where the enchanting story is played on the stage of a magnificent garden which interlaces architectural design and natural growth in a fascinating totality.[7] This is the cult of garden and nature which became reality in the social life of the French aristocracy during the time of Francis I and Henry II. We see it delineated in a beautiful, large, still unknown drawing which I discovered among the treasures of the Cabinet des Dessins in the Louvre (Fig. 61). Horseback riders and hawkers arrive at a garden festivity. Noblemen greet with grand gestures ladies accompanied by pet dogs like the little Peloton whose eulogy was sung by Joachim du Bellay in a charming poem. Clipped hedges, tunnels, and domes of living foliage lead into the depth of the garden. Singers, lute players, musicians, and banqueters populate them. Despite the general gaiety of the scene, the figures have the same Gothic slenderness and almost spectral haughtiness which we notice in the works done by the Italian Mannerists for this society — a secret Gothic. And this society is the same which is sung of in the works of the French lyrical poets, in which the imagery of the painters became word and musical sound. Clément Marot portrayed it in the following verses:

> Mais soulz belle umbre en chambre et galeries
> Nous pourmenons, livres et railleries,
> Dames et bains, seroient les passetemps,
> Lieux et labeurs de nos espritz contens.[8]

Clément Marot forms a beginning. He not only admired Petrarch and Boccaccio but also attempted to translate Vergil, Ovid, and Catullus. We are in the time of Erasmus whose *Adagia* was printed in Paris. Medieval naïveté still slips into Marot's classicality. In the poem on his own childhood "L'enfance de Marot" he describes the charms of the French countryside in a way which suggests the calendar illustrations in the illuminated books. We mentioned before that in the works of his patroness Marguerite of Navarre a similar naïve feeling of nature prevails. A long narrative poem entitled "The Coach" describes how she rides into the open country, enjoying valley and forest, talking to simple people. Three noble ladies emerge from the forest and utter their amorous complaints. They do this in such a rhetorical length and shed so many tears that they charge the sky with the moisture of clouds, and a heavy shower finally pours down, breaking up the elegiac party (Fig. 63). In spite of the cloudburst, they leave the rustic stage in a very dignified manner to join the coach. The great illustrator Bernard Salomon has represented this scene in a delicate little woodcut which adorns Jean de Tournes' edition of Marguerite's poems.[9]

In this early phase of French Renaissance, nature and antiquity go side by side, intermingled in a casual, piecemeal way as in the Netherlandish painting of the early sixteenth century. A real fusion of both to a new imaginative totality did not come about before the Pléiade. The Pléiade was a group of seven likeminded poets and scholars of the era of Henry II, who took this name from the sign of the zodiac. They were led by Pierre de Ronsard and Joachim du Bellay as stars of first order, whereas Remi Belleau,

Jean-Antoine de Baïf, Estienne Jodelle, Jean Daurat, and Pontus de Thyard were the *stellae minores*.

The poetry of the Pléiade is distinguished by two main features: In the first place, it is learned, scholarly poetry which develops its proper artistic and linguistic program, and establishes a poetical theory with definite principles. It follows up a *literary ideal*. In all these respects it may be compared with the works of the painters of the School of Fontainebleau, who were scholarly artists following rules and principles, and who appealed to the taste of educated connoisseurs. In the second place, owing to the superior mastery of its representatives, the poetry of the Pléiade was able to vivify the scholarly achievements. They remained no dead archeological requisites, but became the vehicle of a new attitude toward life imbued with poetical spirit. This poetical enhancement and elevation made human nature, scenery, mythology, past and present appear in a different light — not as facts of a firmly established hierarchic order, but as reflections of the creative poetical mind.

The poets of the Pléiade acquired a thorough knowledge of ancient languages and literature. Ronsard studied Greek with the Hellenist Daurat. Homer, Pindar, Vergil, Ovid, Horace, Tibullus, Propertius, and the great Italians were the models. The poets of the Pléiade held in contempt the old poets of ballads who worked "only by nature, without art and doctrine." They introduced the Alexandrine. The ode and the sonnet were among their favorite forms of poetry. Yet they actively opposed the humanists who believed they could write like Greeks and Romans. Their aim was to regenerate the French language that it might acquire a flexibility and expressiveness matching the ancients. Du Bellay published in 1549 his *Défense et Illustration de la Langue Française*, the theoretical creed of the group in which we read the following sentence: "I cannot blame too strongly the rashness of some of our countrymen, who being anything rather than Greeks or Latins, depreciate and reject everything written in French." The native language should acquire a musical perfection, and Ronsard's poems indeed were favored as texts by sixteenth-century composers.

Marot in his poem "L'enfer" had already described a world of ancient deities which is reminiscent of the Gallery of Francis I. Pleading before Minos, the judge of the dead, the poet enumerates all the pagan deities to whom he is known:

> En la mer suis connu des plus hauts dieux,
> Jusqu'aux Tritons et jusqu'aux Néréides
> En terre aussi des Faunes et Hymnides
> Connu je suis. Connu je suis d'Orphée,
> De mainte nymphe et mainte noble fée.

The subjects of the frescoes of the Gallery pass by in this poem. But it was not until Ronsard that poetry depicted the ancient deities in that lofty, elevated style which we know from the paintings of Fontainebleau. In the verses of a festival entitled "Les Sereines," performed at the canal of Fontainebleau, Ronsard made the pagan deities mix with earthly men, as many a painting of the Fountainebleau School shows:

> Quand nos ayeuls n'estoyent tels que nous sommes,
> Apparoissoyent les Nymphes et les Dieux,
> Et sans avoir une voile sur les yeux,
> Ne desdaignoyent la presence des hommes.
> Par les forests les Sylvains habitoyent,
> Et sur les monts dansoyent les Oreades;
> La mer avoit son Glauque et son Neptun,
> Desur les bords venoit jouer Portun,
> Et les ruisseaux abondoyent des Naiades.

The most cherished object of this poetical cult was Diana, the virgin goddess, tall, slender, youthful, who roamed through the forests. She, her maidens and nymphs embody a new canon of beauty, blending feminine with masculine features, a canon celebrated by Primaticcio in endless variations. Francesco Primaticcio of Bologna had arrived in 1532, and became the artistic dictator in Fontainebleau after Rosso's death. With him, the current of Italian Mannerism which derives from Raphael and the Roman School entered French art. He had worked for six years under Giulio Romano at the Palazzo del Té in Mantua. Primaticcio was a universally gifted artist, an inventive genius of great style. His canon of forms dominated Fontainebleau in the second phase, and through it Europe. From the middle of the sixteenth century onward, Fontainebleau became the center and source of power of many Italianizing trends in Northern European art.

Primaticcio replaced the expressive harshness of Rosso with an elongated, languishing grace. This is the beauty which Ronsard praised in his verses on Eurymedon and Callirrhoe,[10] who was changed into a well in the forest:

> Je voudrois ce jourd'huy, par bonne destinée,
> Me changer d'homme en femme, ainsi que fit Coenée,
> Coenée qui tournant par miracle sa peau,
> Estoit tantost pucelle, et tantost jouvenceau.
> Je verrois dans le baing la belle Callirée:
> Je faux, mais je verrois la belle Cytherée.

Diana, the maidenly goddess, surprised by Actaeon while bathing with her nymphs, was a standard topic of the artists and poets.

> O beau crystal murmurant,
> Que le ciel est azurant
> D'une belle coleur blue,
> Où ma Dame toute nue
> Lave son beau teint vermeil
> Qui retenoit le Soleil . . .

sings Ronsard in Ode XIII of "Le Cinquiesme Livre des Odes." Primaticcio decorated the bathing apartments in Fontainebleau with murals representing this subject; we know the composition from original drawings (Fig. 65). Artificial grottos, like the "Grotte des Pins," were erected in the garden under the poetical device of "Diana's bathing place." [11] The tall, slender, long-legged female type occurs as well in the works of Jean Goujon which represent the style of Fontainebleau in French sculpture. Famous is his group of Diana with the Hart which he did from 1547 to 1549 for the Fountain of the Nymphs in the Castle Anet, the residence of Diane de Poitiers, mistress of Henry II.

As Mannerism liked the elegant, floating, balancing grace of figure, it also liked the ambiguous, changing character of shape. Permutations, transformations were quite to its taste, and therefore, subjects from Ovid's *Metamorphoses* were much in favor. Bernard Salomon's illustrations to Ovid of 1557 charmingly show how human and animal shapes change into trees and bushes. The poetical story of Prince Ciparisse of Cyprus [12] recounts how the boy adorned his favorite animal, a tame hart, with gold and flowers. He killed it by mistake while hunting. As he could not live without the animal, Apollo transformed both into trees.

The two largest works which Primaticcio did in Fontainebleau were the Gallery of Ulysses (destroyed in the eighteenth century) and the large ball room, both completed in the era of Henry II who followed Francis I in 1547 on the throne. Primaticcio adorned the spandrels with mythological frescoes, for the execution of which he had already used the help of the third outstanding Italian painter working in Fontainebleau, Niccolo dell'Abbate, who had arrived in 1552 and introduced the precious Mannerism of Parmiggianino. There the decorative splendor of Primaticcio's style comes to full development. The Wedding Feast of Peleus and Thetis, where Discord throws the apple amid the guests, presents the banqueters most effectfully grouped in the triangular space. Primaticcio's drawings surpass even the executed frescoes in beauty.

A speciality of French court life of the sixteenth century were the festivals, the so-called Masquerades, performed in the halls of the palace or in the open air of the park. Rosso and Primaticcio were the producers who delivered the design not only for the whole setting but for every archaeological and costume detail. Ronsard wrote the verses which the mythological characters had to recite. Occasional poems of this kind form a considerable portion of his work. What these performances were like we may guess not only from costume designs, but also from Primaticcio's drawing for a fresco in the Chambre of the Duchesse d'Étampes, representing Alexander's Masquerade in Persepolis (Fig. 66). The actors pass by with stilted, tiptoeing steps, a solemn choir of tall flaming figures rising to heaven in fantastic disguise which is supposed to be ancient, but is imaginary and fanciful like antiquity in Ronsard's poetry.

We mentioned before that the poets of the Pléiade tried to evoke from scholarly achievements a genuine poetical spirit, and gain new poetical aspects of life. This comes to the fore most vividly in the lyrical poems, in which the poet strips off the ancient cothurnus, and just pours the mood of his soul, tuned by surroundings and scenery, into verses. The feeling of nature, expressed there, is of pagan serenity, at the same time related to the late medieval enjoyment of nature. There, the spirit of Fontainebleau turns completely French and national. I should like to quote some of Ronsard's odes — this, for example, on the selection of his tomb (Livre IV, Ode IV):

> Antres, et vous, fontaines
> De ces roches hautaines
> Qui tombez contre-bas
> D'un glissant pas,
>
> Et vous, forests et ondes
> Par ces prez vagabondes
> Et vous, rives et bois,
> Oyez ma vois.

In art also the style of the School of Fontainebleau gradually became a national French manner, as we see in the picturesque woodcut of a fountain in Auvergne by Bernard Salomon (Fig. 64), almost an illustration of Ronsard's Ode.[13] Another artist in whose art the international style of Fontainebleau turned specifically French was Jean Cousin the Younger, whose *œuvre* of drawings the author was able to reconstruct from many scattered sketches wrongly attributed to various Italian and Netherland masters.[14] A rich pen drawing in the Albertina, delicately washed with purple, places the story of Diana and Endymion in an enchanting bosquet with curly trees, much in the style of the Dutch painter Jan van Scorel, whom Francis I tried in vain to draw to his court. This bosquet is like Ronsard's Forest de Gastine:

> Tes bocages soient tousjours pleins
> D'amoureuses brigades,
> De Satyres et de Sylvains,
> La crainte des Naïades.
>
> En toy habite desormais
> Des Muses le college,
> Et ton bois ne sente jamais
> La flame sacrilege.

Diana as goddess of the moon, "torch bearer, only heir and daughter of the shadows of the night," was sung of in sonnets by Remi

Belleau and Louise Labbé, a poetess who wrote love songs of
wonderful depth.

The profoundest poet of the Pléiade was Joachim Du Bellay,
who admiring the antiquities of Rome consumed himself in nos-
talgia for his native Anjou. Walter Pater devoted one of his finest
studies to him.[15] Du Bellay's visions of scenery are perhaps the
most poetical and soulful ones. When we look at the painting of
The Harvest in Fontainebleau (Fig. 62) where a courtly couple
enjoys the rustic life in the open, windswept country, it brings to
our mind Du Bellay's "Song of a Winnower of Wheat to the
Winds":

> A vous, troupe légère,
> Qui d'aile passagère
> Par le monde volez,
> Et d'un sifflant murmure
> L'ombrageuse verdure
> Doucement ébranlez,
>
> J'offre ces violettes,
> Ces lis et ces fleurettes,
> Et ces roses ici,
> Ces vermeillettes roses,
> Tout fraîchement écloses,
> Et ces œillets aussi.
>
> De votre douce haleine
> Éventez cette plaine,
> Éventez ce séjour,
> Cependant que j'ahanne
> A mon blé que je vanne
> A la chaleur du jour.

The splendid and festive trend of the ancient revival which
stands out so conspicuously in France's artistic and literary culture
of the sixteenth century was not the only, nor even always the
dominating, one. It went parallel to another, equally strong,
equally important — the revival of the medieval spirit. We took
occasion to point out the secret Gothic tendency in the Mannerism of the School of Fontainebleau, the rebirth of the fifteenth-
century enjoyment of nature in the lyrical poetry. Without doubt,
both trends influenced each other strongly. The medieval tradition was never completely interrupted. Yet the Gothic trend in

French art and literature was more than a shadowy afterlife of a bygone era. The mysticism of Marguerite of Navarre, the powerful versification of the Psalms by Marot prove a newly awakened interest in the religious spirit of the Middle Ages. We saw similar trends in the other European countries. In a gloomy poem, "La Mort aux Hommes," Marot makes Death speak to man as in the Gothic danses macabres, murals in the French cemeteries. The poem begins with the verses:

> Incontinent que la mort entendit
> Que l'on voulait inutile la dire,
> Son bras tout sec en arrière étendit,
> Et fièrement son dard mortel brandit,
> Pour République en frapper par grande ire. . . .

With these verses who would not think of Ligier Richier's Epitaph for René de Chalon in the Church of St. Pierre at Bar-le-Duc? Death appears there in the terrifying realism of a skeleton alive. And death speaks to man in Marot's poem:

> L'âme est le feu, le corps est le tison;
> L'âme est d'en haut, et le corps inutile
> N'est autre cas qu'une basse prison
> En qui languit l'âme noble et gentille. . . .

A longing for the beyond, for that which the Middle Ages considered the only good, speaks in these verses. They clearly prove the dual influence of thought under which the French poets and artists worked. The serious note of the transitoriness of earthly pleasures was often sounded by the poets of the Pléiade too, especially by Du Bellay. The revived medieval spirit found its most grandiose expression in the works of Jean Duvet, a goldsmith and engraver who was born in 1485 and died after 1561. Duvet had studied the masters of the Renaissance in Italy. He was acquainted with the works of Leonardo, Mantegna, and Raphael. His grammar of forms fits well into that of the Renaissance of Francis I's era. But how different is the spirit to which these forms are subservient! Duvet's compositions completely disregard all natural or rational space relations. They are patternlike, crowded in a medieval horror vacui like tapestries or sixteenth-century enamels, a kind of work Duvet executed as well. Even poetical subjects, like The Story of the Unicorn,[16] offer a strange dreamlike aspect, unreal and heavy like a nightmare. His greatest and most expressive work is the Apocalypse [17] which he engraved on order of Francis I and Henry II in the years 1546 to 1555. The medieval grandeur of Dürer's Apocalypse inspired these engravings, yet they have a visionary power quite their own. The angel who stands with columns of fire on sea and earth makes the Evangelist swallow the book. His body concretes from billowy clouds; his head sends a cross of rays into space which is constricted by rising rocks, trees, palaces, floating ships, and angels, one above the other in a dreamlike profusion. Even Dürer tried to make real the unreal, in order to make it convincing. Duvet seems to deprive classical Renaissance forms of all real effects, as, for instance, extension in space, logical connection, tectonic accents. The seven-headed dragon which carries the Babylonic harlot on his back rises like lingering columns of smoke. The flaming cities and the wondering men are pressed into the intervals wherever uncovered space gaped. Oppressive peril, threatening cataclysm, and conflagration of the world impend. William Blake's visions are anticipated. The Vision of the Seven Candlesticks (Fig. 68) roars with the swings of ellipses and circles. The mystical intersections of the circuits of celestial bodies rather than Southern tectonics are the ruling laws of this composition. The figures are swerving ornaments instead of tactile solids, but ornaments which speak, which express something — fear, terror, majesty, but also glowing fervor and soothing grace.

Nothing can be compared to the arousing visionariness of Duvet's works except a few things in Old German art. Yet they must have found a deep response in the contemporary mind. The Gothic craving for expression is indelible in Northern art. It breaks through even in the work of a foreigner like the somber, pathetic Lamentation for Christ which Il Rosso painted for the Castle of Écouen shortly before his death.

The Gothic trend in French Renaissance art increased in the second half of the sixteenth century and finally reached its climax about 1600. The more the serenity of spirit which dominated the era of Francis I was replaced by a serious, contemplative, mournful mood, the general mood of the Western world in the era of

Counter Reformation, the more the shadows of the Middle Ages raised their gigantic heads. The body is a prison from which the soul longs to be freed. The enjoyment of physical beauty and nature recedes. If the forms transcend nature, it is not in order to obey a canon of beauty, but to convey expression of soul, depth of sentiment. The light which illuminates the way of men is not sun and moon shining on bosquets with nymphs and fauns, but the light of religion, of faith, of the beyond, the light which shines with a supernatural glare at the end of the long dark tunnel of earthly life. This feeling found its strongest expression in France in the sculptures of Germain Pilon, in the etchings and drawings of Jacques Bellange, and in the writings of St. François de Sales.

Germain Pilon, born in 1535, had passed through Fontainebleau in his youth.[18] He carved several decorative sculptures for the garden. Yet in contrast to Goujon, whose main works were of profane character and served decorative purposes, Pilon struck the serious and solemn note in the style of Fontainebleau. So he turned to ecclesiastic and funereal sculpture. From 1560 to 1563 he carved the three genii who carry the urn with the embalmed heart of Henry II (Louvre). Pilon's works keep a royal pomp, especially the large tombs, but they grow in devout somberness, expressiveness, and realism. Medieval qualities increasingly penetrate the Renaissance nobility. These sculptures are mementos of the vanity of earthly splendor. The tomb of Valentine Balbiani (Louvre), begun in 1572, shows the deceased in her most beautiful array, accompanied by her little pet dog, resting on the slab;[19] a bas-relief on the sarcophagus represents her in repelling realism, lying in the coffin, naked, a decaying corpse, almost a skeleton. The large tomb of Henry II and Catherine de Medici in the Abbey Church of St. Denis, on which Pilon worked from 1563 to 1570, shows the deceased in their royal state kneeling on the platform of the chapel. Inside, they lie naked on the pall, stripped of all their splendor, human wrecks like any poor beggar. The realism has the sole purpose of directing the minds of the onlookers towards the beyond. Akin to El Greco in spirit is the Mater Dolorosa in the Church of St. Paul in Paris, perhaps the most sublime and spiritualized work of this greatest French sculptor of the century (Fig. 67).[20] Out of a mass of drapery, the noble, straight silhouette of her body frees itself, rising like a Gothic tower. Her head is bent in silent mourning. There, the most beautiful works of French Gothic come to life again. As ecstatic in expression is the kneeling St. Francis in the Church St. Jean-St. François. He receives the stigmata, enraptured in sacred inspiration, giving up himself to the vision of the Crucified. The marble seems to be pervaded by an inner light, the light of religious fervor and devotion. Both works were done in the 1580's, and are worthy contemporaries of El Greco's altar paintings.

The highest degree of spiritualization, of expressive transformation of reality, and estrangement from nature was reached in the art of Jacques Bellange. It is the very quintessence of Mannerism, refined to the utmost subtlety and losing all earthly weight. Bellange's figures seem to glide like flames over the ground without touching it. We know little about his life. Bellange was court painter to the Duke of Lorraine. His traceable activity covers the years from 1602 to 1619. He was a belated artist working far into the seventeenth century, which followed up ideals different from his. His work was a late fruit of Mannerism — this may explain its unmatched expressive refinement. He executed decorative paintings for the Palace of Nancy and altarpieces for the churches of the city. Nothing has survived of them; only the delightful proofs of his draughtsmanship and graphic art are preserved. The decorative paintings of festivals and masquerades followed the program of Fontainebleau. Yet we may assume from the drawings that all features of classical beauty in them were distorted as in a magic mirror to a fantastic, ghostlike world.[21] Figures seem to be no longer those of human beings, but of exotic flowers and plants. They palpitate and flare.

The same strangeness of form was applied by Bellange to his religious works. The final aim of this Mannerism was not a superficial play of formal devices, but expression of soul, as tender and delicate as may be imagined. An admirable red chalk drawing in the Albertina (Fig. 69) shows the Three Marys at the Sepulcher, mystical souls whose subtle emotions are revealed in the touch of their long fingers. They are the very embodiment of that beauty of the soul of which St. François de Sales wrote in his *Philothée* or *Introduction à la Vie devote*, published in 1609.[22] Philothée is a noble lady whom the Saint instructs in keeping the soul untouched amid the conventions of social life and directed towards the higher spiritual realm. She is taught how to meditate, to place herself in presence of the Lord, to purify herself from affectations. The tendency of this book is toward a mystical yielding to God, as glowing and boundless as that of the great mystics of the fourteenth century, yet more intimate, more personal, keeping within the framework of style and fashion of the time. We may imagine Philothée to be like one of the three damosels who converse with the angel at the tomb after the Resurrection.[23] They rise like strange tulips in the Lord's flower garden. Their coiffures, their flowing silk robes accord with the taste of the time. The small heads are burdened with fluffy wigs, the hands twist in precious gestures. Do these mundane traits mean a profanation of a sacred subject? Far from that. In their courtly exquisiteness, they are intended to impart the miraculous, mysterious, supernatural of the holy event. The perfume of their beautiful souls extinguishes the difference of coarse matters. Nude skin and garment merge into one unity which is neither flesh nor cloth but a new purified substance, an emanation of the mystical feeling. Religious art of the international style about 1400 produced similar forms.

In the large etching The Carrying of the Cross,[24] a mighty choir of such extravagant figures rises, weightless and uncorporeal, like pouring columns of smoke, out of which faces emerge as if seen in a dream. Bellange had been in Italy, and learned from the works of the Sienese Mannerists who presented similar mystical tendencies, but his boundless subjectivism dismissed the last vestiges of formal logic indispensable with Italian art.

The art of Bellange in its expressive climax seems to bring about the very last fulfillment of Mannerism as the penetration of the ancient revival with the spirituality of the Middle Ages.

VIII

Related Trends in Arts and Sciences of the Late Renaissance

I F WE inquire which intellectual force grew strongest in Europe at the end of the sixteenth century, we shall find that it was neither art nor religion, neither poetry nor humanism that answered the most burning questions of the cultural world. This task was fulfilled by the same power which dominated Europe undisputedly in the seventeenth century, *science*. The era of science began to eclipse the era of art. It was science not in the intuitive form of the pantheistic thinkers of the first half of the sixteenth century, but science in the most intellectual and exact form: astronomy, mathematics, and anthropology.

One can read, mainly in older textbooks, that the late phase of the sixteenth century with which we have to deal in this last chapter is sometimes called "Early Baroque." This is incorrect. We shall see in the analysis of the works of art which we are going to discuss that their basic formal structure is *Manneristic*. We have become acquainted with Mannerism as the stylistic expression of the epoch of Late Renaissance, an epoch which lasted very long, especially in Northern Europe. It lasted longer there than in the Italian South, because Mannerism, as we have seen, implies a certain resuscitation of Gothic transcendence and expressiveness — values to which the North always inclined in accordance with its characteristic mental disposition. While in Italy Caravaggio's powerful realism put an end to Mannerism in the first years of the seventeenth century, it still survived in the rest of Europe, blending with the beginnings of the Baroque in a kind of twilight [1] which brings to our mind the blending of Late Gothic and Renaissance in the Netherlands a hundred years before. Therefore, it is justified if we extend the time-limit of our consideration into the beginning of the seventeenth century.

A few words should be said about the method of approach to

the problem in this chapter. We know very well that there is no absolute progress in the history of art. Artistic values grow and shrink in succeeding periods. The artistic genius incessantly produces new forms while others die off. Yet the development of science is considered as a continuous way upward. No achievement is considered as incapable of being improved and carried further by the following generation. This mental attitude toward the history of science is mainly due to the circumstance that we ourselves live in a rising era of science where life, for good or bad, is increasingly shaped by scientific progress. But the fact that scientific achievements obtained by antiquity decayed or were lost in the Middle Ages, ought to make us consider that a repetition of this process is by no means impossible, and also that the development of science may be more subject to the laws of historical growth and decay than nowadays we are inclined to believe. It is difficult to imagine that one field alone of the cultural activity of man may be exempted from those laws to which all others are subservient. Therefore, it seems not inappropriate to reason that the history of science has its different phases and periods of style like all other achievements of the human race. It is not accidental which mathematical and scientific problems arise at a given period. At least the setting up of problems is subject to historical change, even in the field of mathematics and exact sciences. The history of ideas teaches us that the same spiritual factors underlie the various cultural activities. Hence, its method permits us to draw parallels between artistic and scientific phenomena, and to expect mutual illumination therefrom.

The astronomy of the sixteenth century was overshadowed by the tremendous discovery of Copernicus, published in his *De Revolutionibus Orbium Celestium Libri VI* in 1543.[2] We can imagine how deeply the discovery that the earth was no longer the center of the universe, the firm basis of all things which it had been since Ptolemy, but that it freely circled in space round the sun may have affected the human mind. "In the midst of all dwells the Sun. For who could set this luminary in another or better place in this most glorious temple than whence he could at once and the same time lighten the whole? . . . And so, as if seated upon a royal throne, the Sun rules the family of the planets as they circle round him. . . ." [3] (Fig. 1). Copernicus achieved the theoretical formulation of a notion of space which developed at about the same time in painting from Altdorfer to Bruegel — a notion of space which suggests the grandeur of the universe by man's eccentric position in it.

Although Copernicus removed the earth from its central position and built the cosmos around the sun as center, he did not

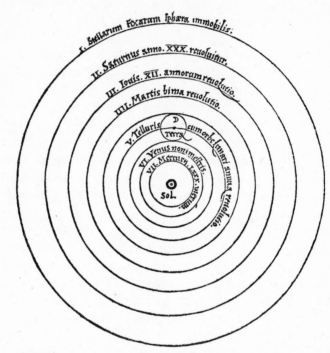

I. COPERNICUS: THE SPHERIC STRUCTURE OF THE UNIVERSE

change the ruling idea of the cosmic space itself. This idea regarded cosmic space as a series of seven concentric spheres of solid crystal-clear substance. Each sphere contains one of the great planets firmly anchored in its perfect round. The outermost spheric husk is studded with the multitude of the fixed stars. According to this notion, the universe is something perfectly spheric in shape, yet limited. We find this notion of the limited universe visualized in a drawing of the Last Judgment done in 1555 by the Westphalian painter Hermann tom Ring (Fig. 70).[4] It is a dramatic work, filled with Michelangelesque nudes in wild motion, representing the struggle between the resurrected and the demons. The universe is shown as the interior of a tremendous solid dome. Its vault is cut by a circular opening; the lid sinks down and hangs freely in the air carrying Mary, St. John, and the Angels who announce the Last Day. Christ floats on the globe as a separate little sphere. Above him hovers a ring with angels who hold the instruments of the Passion, rotating around the dove of the Holy Ghost. Beyond the inner circle with the figures of the Apostles extends an amphitheater of blessed souls. This building of concrete supplants the usual ranges of clouds. It is supplemented by a spiral staircase on which the blessed souls mount to heaven.

This drawing is an instructive example of the way in which art and science in history are linked with each other. *The creative mind at a given historical moment thinks in certain forms which are the same in arts and sciences.*

We meet this notion of the universe as a concrete cosmic building in an earlier painting by Hieronymus Bosch representing the Assumption of the Blessed Souls to Paradise.[5] In it a long dark tunnel breaks through the husk of the cosmic sphere and opens into a magic realm of light beyond.

Thinking in terms of mathematically defined space increased in arts and sciences in the second half of the sixteenth century. After the medieval complexity, the Copernican system had brought simplification. The courses of the planets seen from the earth describe strange loops, which astronomy since Ptolemy had tried to explain through the assumption of epicycles, cycles described by the planets around their main circuits, the deferents, while moving along. Copernicus' theory replaced this intricacy by a great simplification which answered the aesthetic striving of High Renaissance art for balance and harmony. On the other hand, it rooted up the geocentric anchor hold of man and threw him out into the space of the universe. The ground yielded, and man hovered in bottomless space. We can well understand that a firmly established church, whether Catholic or Protestant, would violently oppose the new theory as something threatening all divine stability. This feeling is conveyed by a composition of Jacopo Tintoretto, painted in 1548, five years after the publication of

Copernicus' book, which represents the miraculous rescue of a Christian slave by St. Mark. The main figure falls upside down into the picture space like a messenger from another celestial body with opposite gravity. Everything seems to totter. The figures are poised in contrasting diagonals and no longer have the firm hold on the earthly ground which they had in the High Renaissance compositions.

To shape *space* is one of the foremost artistic problems. From static space it becomes increasingly curved, dynamic, potential space. We can follow this development in Bruegel's dealing with the subject of the Tower of Babel. In 1563, he painted the picture now in the Museum of Vienna. The tower grows out of natural rock, and is already reaching into the clouds, throwing a gigantic shadow over land and sea. One story is superimposed upon the other in solid balance. Where the building is incomplete, its inner structure becomes visible, seemingly inspired by the Colosseum which the painter had seen in Rome. The tower which we observe from a hill seems to incline to fall out of space toward us. This inclination increases the feeling of space as much as it impairs the stability. In a later version, Bruegel diminished the stability still more (Fig. 72).[6] Without any foothold, we hover over the scenery. This tower is taller and more slender in proportions, and screws itself up into the clouds in a dynamic spiral. We saw a similar spiral form in Hermann tom Ring's Last Judgment. This later version found so many repetitions in Manneristic paintings of the late sixteenth century that it must have appealed more to the ruling taste than the earlier one. It proves that the High Renaissance stability was replaced in the second half of the century by more complicated kinetics. We shall see something similar in science.[7]

The late sixteenth century was an era of an internationality which can only be compared to the early and high Middle Ages. While Netherlanders, Frenchmen, and Germans traveled to Italy, Italians traveled to the North, all finding esteem and commissions abroad. The court of Emperor Rudolph II in Prague gathered Netherlandish, Italian, German, and Scandinavian artists and scientists. The stylistic language of Manneristic art was as international as Manneristic culture was. It centered mostly at the courts, and court culture has always been international.[8] For this reason, I cannot confine myself to limited national areas in Northern Europe, but have also to include Italy and Spain in my account. This chapter, therefore, is a review of all the cultural regions of the preceding ones.

None of the professional scientists conceived so daring and prophetic an idea of the universe as did the greatest philosopher of science in the second half of the century, Giordano Bruno. Bruno was a fervent advocate of the Copernican system, but he eliminated the idea of the universe as a limited sphere and established it as the unlimited space filled with countless celestial bodies, with fiery suns and cold watery moons which receive their light from the suns, with fixed stars and planets whose movements we cannot observe because of their remoteness. He developed this idea with artistic intuition mainly in the "Dialogues on the Infinite, Universe and Worlds" (Venice, 1584) [9] and in the satirical dialogue "The Ash-Wednesday Feast." [10] We read in the latter the following sentences: "We comprehend that there is only *one* sky, *one* infinite ether in which those resplendent lumina keep their lawful distances in order to participate in the eternal life. Those flaming celestial bodies are the ambassadors who glorify the sublimity and majesty of God!"

Three years after these words were written, the aged Tintoretto began to paint the Paradise in the Sala del Gran Consiglio of the Ducal Palace in Venice (Fig. 73).[11] According to the order of the Litany, the Angels, Saints, and Blessed in increasingly larger circles range themselves around the Virgin who is praying before the Saviour as the center. They are freely hovering and revolving celestial bodies, who perform lawful, mathematically exact motions, radiant from an inner light, each one animated and driven by his own spiritual power.[12] The space of the universe is filled with countless figures. A passage from the "Dialogues on the Infinite, Universe and Worlds" says: "If the majesty of God is bound to develop in innumerable degrees of perfection, so it is necessary that there are countless individua, and such are those great animated beings to whom our earth belongs, our divine mother who has borne us, who sustains us and will receive us again. For the reception of those countless celestial bodies, an infinite space is required." [13] Here, without any doubt, painting and scientific thought have expressed the same profound idea. We do not need to assume a direct mutual influence which is rather unlikely, but *these great problems and ideas impregnated the spiritual atmosphere of the time, and found their expression in arts and sciences independently*.

The Venetian master's huge, multifold compositions seem to be ruled by a mechanical regularity and mathematical exactness. The figures of the Resurrection of the Dead which Tintoretto painted in 1560 for his own burial church S. Maria dell'Orto rush up and down, driven by an inner dynamism like the automatic figures of an immense clock. Automatons and clockworks were favored in the era of Mannerism, but not as a mere pastime and amusement, as we might assume from the attention which the aged Charles V devoted to them in the Escorial. This fashion had a deeper spiritual reason: *the automatons mirrored the mechanism of the universe*. We notice here in Tintoretto's art a remarkable similarity to that of Bruegel, a similarity which is dictated by the spirit of the time, and not caused by outer influences.

One can recognize in Tintoretto's paintings certain recurring types of figures in movement, only seen in different aspects. They are not individuals, only embodiments of abstract spiritual motions. They change their significance according to their varying placement like the motives in a musical canon or fugue, which remain the same and change their meaning only by altering their position.

At this time, in Venice and to the North of the Alps, a revival of the polyphony of the late Middle Ages took place in music as much as in the visual arts. Andrea and Giovanni Gabrieli of Venice and the great organ master Claudio Merulo are representatives of this new polyphony which cultivated especially the musical form of the motet. The fugues of the vocal compositions of Mannerism tower up to the altitude of sixteen and twenty voices like the tremendous pictorial inventions of Tintoretto.[14] The Netherlanders, who during the fifteenth century had dominated in the musical field as much as in painting, again played a leading part in this revival of medieval polyphony. The greatest composer of the time was Roland de Lattre of Mons, who Italianized his name to

Orlando di Lasso. He was active at the court of the Duke of Bavaria at Munich, a center of Manneristic art. He handled the style of the worldly madrigal and the spiritual motet with equal virtuosity, making both types of musical composition benefit from each other. He gave a new harmonic meaning to the polyphonic structure, achieving new and surprising effects. He provided the single voices with vigorous accents according to the words of the text, increased their rhythmical articulation and the width of their tonal strides.[15] He made abundant use of chromatics, as we see the painters of the time cultivate iridescent shiftings of colors.

The artistic adviser at the court of Munich in Lasso's time was Frederik Sustris of Amsterdam. We are going to see that the Netherlands gain an increasing importance in the development of the Late Mannerism. A wave of artistic energies swept from the Netherlands over Europe as much as from Italy. In their artistic grammar, the monumental Roman style increasingly changed into elongated, flamboyant, labile forms which not only are reminiscent of Parmiggianino and the School of Fontainebleau, but also bring to new life elements of the art of the Late Gothic Mannerists about 1520. In the field of architectural ornament, the style of Cornelis Floris of Antwerp was dominant.[16] In the interlacement of his designs, we find mathematical exactitude combined with irrational phantasy. This style found a tremendous following in Germany where arts and crafts were attracted by its irrational character. Masonry and décor, furniture and jewelry eagerly absorbed this international style. It is a complicated, brittle, spiny, thorny world of forms which threatens to hurt one wherever one touches it. Here belong the works of the great goldsmith Wenzel Jamnitzer of Nuremberg.[17]

In science we notice a similar tendency toward renewed complexity and refinement. Astronomy became the leading science because it is the science not only of abstract intellectual motions but also of the basic realities in the universe. After the grandiose spatial simplicity of Copernicus' system, Tycho Brahe, the foremost astronomer in the last decades of the century, brought about a new complication. In his book *De Mundi Aetherii Recentioribus Phaenomenis* (1588), he returned to the medieval concept of the earth as the unmoved center of the universe, but he made all the other planets revolve around the sun (Fig. 11). The sun on its part revolved like the moon and the sphere of the fixed stars around the earth as the center. The great concentric harmony of Copernicus was again replaced by a new objective eccentricity, basically dif-

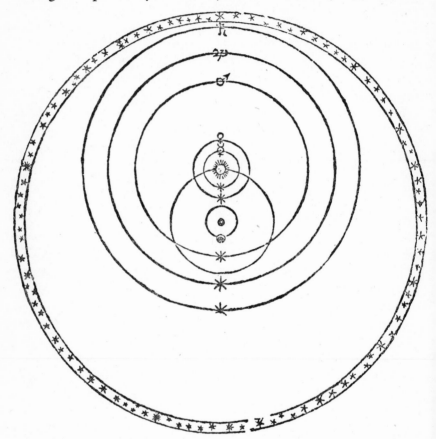

II. TYCHO BRAHE: THE SPHERIC STRUCTURE OF THE UNIVERSE

ferent from the epicycles of the pre-Copernican era, yet nevertheless related to them.[18] This is a scientific parallel to the medieval revival in the fine arts.

The greatest patron of astronomy and mathematics at the end of the sixteenth century was Emperor Rudolph II, who was also the greatest patron of the arts in the North. In his favorite residence, the castle of the Hradshin in Prague, he assembled not only

the most magnificent art collection of his time, but also outstanding painters, sculptors, architects, musicians, mathematicians, and
astronomers. In 1598, Tycho Brahe was called from Denmark to
Prague by the Emperor. This assembly, in spite of its cosmo-
politanism, had a specific character which in the history of art is
designated as the style of the Rudolphinian artists. The Netherlanders had a great share in it.

The leading artist in the group was Bartholomaeus Spranger of
Antwerp, called from Vienna to Prague in 1580. His realm of
forms competes in complexity with the most intricate calculations
of the astronomers and mathematicians. A painting in the museum
of Vienna (Fig. 75) represents Pallas defeating ignorance and pro-
tecting the arts and sciences, among whom astronomy with her
astrolabe stands out. It is a complicated mechanism of labile,
slightly touching, extremely movable forms. They curve through
space in serpentines, parabolas, and hyperbolas.[19] Even the subjects of erotic mythology, very common among those painters,
lose all their nearness to life and become merely compositional
artifacts.

The geometric structure of Spranger's formal concepts is even
more distinct in his pen drawings. In these bold and quick sketches,
the lines dash over the surface with a remarkable spatial grasp, like
the angular distances drawn from the planets to the adjacent stars
which Tycho Brahe measured. The subject matter as such is of
little importance. Whether it is a story of the Old Testament like
Judith and Holofernes,[20] or a mythological subject like Bellerophon
taming the Pegasus,[21] we notice the same brittle, highly dynamic
configurations of lines which resemble the patterns of ice ferns on
a window pane. The figures twist, turn, and sprawl. Apollo with
his lyre, balancing like a dancer (Fig. 76),[22] and Leda with the
swan,[23] behave in the same mannered and affected way. The purpose was not the rendering of nature but the exemplification of
abstract motions.

While Spranger's art is purely formal and void of deeper content, the German Hans von Aachen was capable of a serious religious note. His Lamentation for Christ exhales a great inward
pathos, proper to the transcendental mood of the religious art of
the Counter Reformation.[24] If we look in German art of the late

sixteenth century for something akin in spirit to El Greco and
Bellange, it is found in this drawing. The heads are oblong ovals;
the glances strive toward heaven or are downcast; torches rise in
fumes.

Hans Vredeman de Vries of Leeuwarden belonged as an architect to the group around Rudolph II. He was an ingenious designer
and painter of intricate buildings, pompous halls and arcades, gardens and courtyards. They extend in endless sequences like the
naves of Gothic cathedrals, speculative and abstract, dream castles
which never became reality. They are visual counterparts of the
involved compositions for clavichord and organ of Late Manneristic instrumental music. The Emperor also had composers among
his artists in Prague; Jacobus Gallus and Hans Leo Hasler stand
out among them. This Netherlandish mode dominated almost the
whole of Germany.

We have emphasized how international this artistic culture was.
It is no wonder that this same style ruled in the Netherlandish
homelands at the end of the sixteenth century. The Venetians,
mainly Tintoretto, were the leading influence. The artists now
went as frequently to Venice as to Rome. Maerten de Vos of
Antwerp had even been a pupil and collaborator of Tintoretto.
In his Last Judgment in the museum of Seville, he crowded the
picture space with a confusing abundance of figures in the most
varying sizes. As in the paintings of El Greco, large figures are
juxtaposed to very small ones, and so suggest spatial tension.

Holland fostered more fascinating artists than Flanders at the
end of the century. Haarlem and Utrecht were centers of artistic
activity. In Haarlem, the so-called Haarlem Academicians [25] developed their style; they were more outstanding as draughtsmen
and engravers than as painters. As the name of their group indicates, the study of the nude took great prominence in their artistic
program. Cornelis Cornelissen mastered it with greatest virtuosity,
cramming difficult foreshortenings and wrenched poses into his
inventions, as the drawing of the Brazen Serpent of 1599 in Oxford [26] proves. Hendrik Goltzius was the most outstanding engraver of his time, a master of his craft who underwent a severe
training, emulating the great artists of the past, Dürer and Lucas
van Leyden. A retrospective tendency toward the masters of Late

Gothic and Early Renaissance is very significant with those artists. Nevertheless, they were more than mere archaists and eclectics; they were very modern and progressive artists. The Standard Bearer (Bartsch, no. 125) by Goltzius (1589) is one of his proudest and most ostentatious works, full of sparkling brilliancy and bouncing elasticity.[27] We find in it formal principles similar to those in the works of Spranger which Goltzius reproduced in some of his engravings.

The painters of Utrecht excelled in intricate figure compositions for which the Olympus by Joachim van Uytewael in the Museum of Braunschweig is exemplary.[28] Heavy clouds bulge like celestial bodies on which numerous nudes elegantly twist and balance — a sophisticated automaton world in unnatural colors. A more fascinating painter was Abraham Bloemaert. The complete mastering of centrifugal, radiating, and eruptive elements did not hinder him from imbuing his paintings with a stirring dramatic spirit like the Judith in the Museum of Vienna,[29] showing the head of Holofernes to the Jewish people by torchlight at night. Brilliant reds, blues, greens, and yellows flare up like rockets in the blackish darkness. Figures appear in surprising poses and at capricious distances.

These artists display a dexterity and virtuosity in their works which we also find in contemporary music, for instance in the compositions for clavichord and organ by Jan Pietersz Sweelinck of Amsterdam.

The Dutch Late Renaissance masters, besides being virtuosi of artificial composition, were also powerful interpreters of the image of man. Anthropology as the science of the conduct of life gained increasing importance. Then, the Dutch philologists worked on the revival of Stoic philosophy, the aim of which was a deeper understanding of the human character and the gaining of principles for the right conduct of life. Michel de Montaigne, Joseph Justus Scaliger, and Justus Lipsius in their writings strove for a true and faithful notion of man, as we also see it in the masterly portraits by Antonis Mor of Utrecht who spent many years as official portraitist at the Spanish court and thus gained international importance. The portrait which he painted of William the Silent (Gallery of Cassel) is the most impressive effigy of this great historical character in his taciturnity and faithful constancy. Bruegel's friend, the engraver and religious philosopher Coornhert, who took refuge in Holland from Spanish persecution, was portrayed by Hendrik Goltzius in a large print (Bartsch, no. 164) which brings the stern and vigorous features of this fighter for freedom of spirit most vividly before our eyes. The greatest draughtsman among the Dutch artists was Jacques de Gheyn, a native of Antwerp, who made a most appealing and spontaneous sketch of his wife and his little son who look at father's sketchbook by candlelight.[30]

If we study the art of the late Mannerists, we notice that in spite of increasing involution and artificiality in the general concept, there was a considerable increase in the study of nature and in realism in details. We see this clearly in the works of the landscape painters. Gillis van Coninxloo shows the interior of aboriginal forests, entangled in the intricacy of vegetable forms like the palaces of Vredeman de Vries, glittering in fantastic chiaroscuro. The study of the plants in detail shows the greatest faithfulness to nature. Scientific objectivity grows in the same degree as the irrational complexity of invention.

We notice a similar trend toward careful observation of reality in science. Exact observation is considered as the main quality of Tycho Brahe's work. He increased the exactness of instruments immensely, sometimes by enlarging them to a gigantic scale.[31] He compounded a catalogue of the fixed stars, a topography of the sky, which competed in accuracy with the new mapping of the globe. He was not that type of a scholar who, with an ingenious new concept preconceived in the creative mind, approaches reality and subjects both his concept and reality to renewed tests. This demands a formative genius of the highest potency, a genius who mentally perceives a new idea with an almost visual clarity. Only the greatest geniuses who gave a new turn to the course of science were endowed with this gift.

Such a genius was Johannes Kepler who took up the heritage of Tycho Brahe.[32] Kepler, born in Swabia in 1571, was deeply religious and at first intended to become a theologian. A position as astronomer and mathematician, offered to him in Austria, bound him for almost all his life to that country. He was invited by

Tycho Brahe to Prague in 1600. After Tycho's death he became court astronomer to Emperor Rudolph. He erected a monument to both — his predecessor and to his patron — in the *Tabulae Rudolphinae*.[33]

Kepler himself stated in his book *Harmonices Mundi*[34] that the same basic impulse of the human spirit works in both artistic pleasure and astronomical research. In the pleasure of rhythm and harmony, the spirit is only apparently passive; in reality, it also unfolds there an autonomous motion and activity. The elevation and inspiration of its very essence, which the spirit feels, is at the bottom its own work, to which it is guided not by a conscious intention, but by a natural instinct.

Kepler wrote these words with regard to music, but they are also valid for the visual arts. Astronomy was to Kepler identical with geometry as the visualization of abstract laws. The visual, the aesthetic point of view is already outspoken in his first book entitled *Mysterium Cosmographicum* (1596).[35] He tried to reveal in it the harmonic relations in the construction of the universe. He took the five regular solids from tetrahedron to icosahedron. He inscribed spheres into them and circumscribed spheres around them in growing proportions (Fig. 77).[36] His supposed discovery was that the radii of those spheres are proportional to the distances of the planets from the sun. Stereometric combinations of this kind were frequent in the visual arts of the time. Turners of wood and ivory liked to inscribe geometrical bodies into each other, so that the smaller ones were freely rotating, and yet imprisoned in the larger ones. Jamnitzer published in 1568 a *Perspectiva Corporum Regularium* which displays devices of this kind (Fig. 78).[37]

Kepler discarded Brahe's return to the geocentric concept and reëstablished the Copernican system, but he discovered mistakes and incongruences in Copernicus' calculations. He originated a new theory of the planets and chose as his main topic the course of Mars. In Brahe's observations from 1580 to 1596, this planet had described very "Manneristic" cycloid loops (Fig. 111) which reminded Kepler of a lenten pretzel. Therefore Kepler had to return to the heliocentric system in order to eliminate the movement of the earth. He disclosed the final result in his *Astronomia Nova* (1609).[38] In his introductory dedication to the Emperor he proudly asserts that he has brought the God of War himself, caught in the net of calculi as once Vulcan caught him with Venus, before his patron. This allegory brings before our eyes the muscular, boasting deities of Mannerism. Yet the main importance of the *Astronomia Nova* with regard to the arts lies in the first and

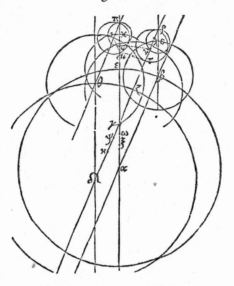

III. JOHANNES KEPLER: EPICYCLE DIAGRAM
ACCORDING TO TYCHO BRAHE

second of the three great Keplerian laws which it contains. The first law states that the circuits of the planets are not circles, but ellipses with two foci in one of which the sun is located (Fig. IV).[39]

From his ingenious vision of form, which was akin to that of the contemporary artists, Kepler was to discover one of the basic laws in the mechanism of the universe. We see everywhere in the art of the late sixteenth century how important ellipses, parabolas, and hyperbolas were for the formal structure. These types of curves purport the approach toward the elongated, the dynamic, the transcendental, away from the self-sufficient, world-embracing circle. The universe from a cosmos becomes a dynamic potential, in art and science alike. Giordano Bruno had already observed that there was no motion in reality which would not deviate considerably from the simple regular circle. The sketch which Tintoretto painted for the Paradise (Fig. 74) [40] goes beyond the executed work which presents sectors of circles. It shows the holy ranges compressed to ellipses; for this reason, it is much more suggestive of *space*. *The conquest of space* is the leitmotiv of all these endeavors. Arithmetic as science of mere numbers was void of con-

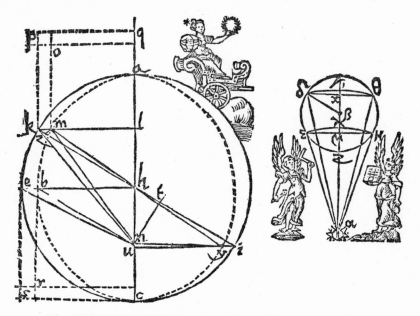

IV. JOHANNES KEPLER: RELATION BETWEEN CIRCLE
AND INSCRIBED ELLIPSIS

tent to Kepler, if it did not refer to geometry, that is, intuition of space. Parabola and hyperbola dynamically and unendingly sweep into the infinite space (Fig. v).[41]

If we turn to the very greatest artists about 1600, we find these basic traits of imagination confirmed everywhere. The Adoration of the Name of Christ with the portrait of Philip II in the Escorial, which El Greco painted for the King as a proof of his art (Fig. 71), shows the celestial universe as a visionary structure of intercrossing rays of light and curves, mathematical and mystical at the same time.[42] Huge ellipses make the host of the angels in heaven and the crowd of the faithful on earth extend into the infinite. The gigantic mouth of hell opens in a huge parabolic silhouette.

The groups in heaven form clusters of rays. The Name of Christ, in centrifugal potency, emits straight lines of light into space along which the adoring angels with their wings and the clouds crystallize. The human form seems to be enchained in a net of mystical geometry, which in El Greco's religious paintings serves the purpose of conquering the transcendental space of the heavenly realm. We see this most strikingly expressed in the famous Burial of Count Orgaz of 1586 in the church of San Tomé in Toledo. The abstract shapes of clouds, supernaturally elongated figures, and canals of light focus in the visionary flaming figure of Christ, and

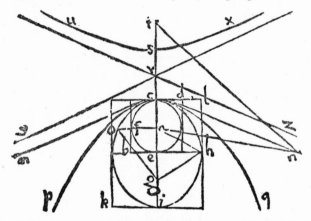

V. JOHANNES KEPLER: CONSTRUCTION OF PARABOLA
AND HYPERBOLA

seem at the same time to eradiate from it. Bodies, faces, and torches in the earthly region flame in a mystical longing toward the beyond. This work is Mannerism in its highest degree of spiritualization. It is completely in the line of Manneristic art if the spectral oblong faces of the mourners reveal the most stupendous portrait realism in detail.

In his latest period, in 1609, El Greco painted a prospect and map of the city of Toledo (Fig. 79). The wide line of horizon stretches beneath a cloudy sky which palpitates with sheet lightning. The silhouette of the city, the track of its walls and buildings, curves from the resting river god at the left in a dynamic spatial sweep toward the asymptote of the horizon without ever reaching it, and dies away in the hilly terrain behind the man who demonstrates the map. The large size of the foreground figures increases the spatial tension. A magnetic dynamism seems to govern this prospect.

Mathematics about this time proceeded from the calculation of given quantities to that of potentials and possibilities. Vieta developed algebra to an international language and applied it to trigonometry.

Kepler knew that the foundation of astronomy could be achieved only in connection with a scientific foundation of physics. His interest turned increasingly toward the notion and the law of energy as a problem. He solved it in the second and third of his laws. The second law states that "the planets run with varying speeds around the sun so that the radius vector drawn from the sun to the planet describes equal areas in equal times." [43] This means that the planet increases its speed the more it approaches the sun on its elliptic course, and slows it up when moving in the opposite direction. The physical explanation which he gave for this dynamism was an *anima motrix*, a source of motion, located in the sun, sending out rays of energy, straight lines of force which hold and carry the planets. He was influenced in this regard by William Gilbert's book *De Magnete*, published in 1600.[44] We see in the works by El Greco how a great painter visualized such lines of force.[45]

We may study the crescendo and decrescendo of energy which Kepler formulated in his second law in the works of the engravers and draughtsmen, too. The Adoration of the Magi,[46] an etching by Jacques Bellange, rebounds from these elastic, highly spiritualized energies which flow through a tense crowd of figures. In elegant curves, they sweep, evade and entangle, flee and pursue each other, in relentless, because magnetic, and not organic, motion.

Bellange etched cycles of saintly figures, including among others the Holy Magi. The figure of the Moorish King Gaspar [47] is not only refined and subtle like the precious vessel which he holds up in such a precious way, but also it moves in that complex, labile balance in which the circulating energies outweigh each other. The ellipse of the beturbaned head flows out in the sweep of a plume.

The drawing of a group of women with children by Bellange in the Louvre (Fig. 80) shows human beings transformed into the most advanced geometrical abstractions. Ellipses and parabolic curves swerve along, growing and fading, making the human organism a configuration of astral energies.

In a more realistic way, we see the same kinetics of line displayed in a grandiose drawing of the Parable of the Sower by Jacques de Gheyn.[48] As the fiend sows the seed of evil, demonic forces brew in the sky and sweep through the masses of clouds in the shapes of witches, like those in Shakespeare's tragedies which the artist may have seen on the stage in England during his stay there.

The idea of the mechanism of the universe which began in art with Tintoretto and Bruegel reached its climax in the scientific system of Kepler. But Kepler replaced the notion of soul, the animism of the earlier thinkers by the notion of physical energy. This did not diminish the transcendental, deeply philosophical and religious character of his thought. While analyzing the works of art, we have often had to refer to music. Kepler himself took the step from science to music. When searching for the deepest reason of the harmony of the universe, he discovered his third great law: "The squares of the periodic times of the several planets are proportional to the cubes of their mean distances from the sun." [49] He published this law in his book *Harmonices Mundi* (1619). He brought this harmony of the spheres in relation to the harmonious sounds. He expressed in musical notes the harmonies and melodies connected with the different planets (Fig. vi). This music of the spheres centers in the idea of the creator. German music has been mathematical, transcendental, and deeply religious from the days of Kepler to those of Johann Sebastian Bach. It is full of an otherworldly optimism. The music of Bach is the gayest of all because it is most confident in God.

Kepler also took up the problems of optics on a geometrical basis,[50] investigating the figures of light and the refractions, problems which played such an important part in painting of the late Mannerism on the eve of the Baroque. He tried to describe the essence of color in terms which Goethe called daring and strange: "Color is light in potency, light buried in translucid substance; different grades in the condition of the substance, its looseness or density, its translucency or darkness, cause the difference of colors." Color as light in potency, as light buried in translucent substance is what we see in the works of Adam Elsheimer, the greatest German painter at the beginning of the seventeenth century, for instance in the Three Marys at the Sepulchre on Easter Morning, in the museum of Bonn.

The problems of light obtained increasing prominence in painting as well as in philosophical and scientific thought. To the philosopher Jacob Boehme, whose ideas derived from Paracelsus, light was a magic power. To the scientist Kepler, color was a

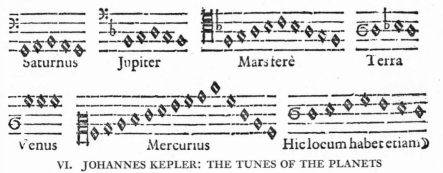

Saturnus Jupiter Mars fere Terra

Venus Mercurius Hic locum haber etiam.

VI. JOHANNES KEPLER: THE TUNES OF THE PLANETS

function of light. The art of the great painters of the seventeenth century, of Rembrandt and Vermeer, brought the final fulfillment of these ideas.

Dürer at the beginning of the Northern Renaissance had freed the realm of spirit from its medieval metaphysical limitations through a new empiricism. Kepler at its close, living exactly one century after Dürer, maintained the sovereignty of the creative spirit over the realm of empirical experience.

The transcendental and the empirical world contributed equally to the ideological structure of the sixteenth century. The rational was limited to the matter of empirical experience. Kepler widened the reach of reason to the sphere of the speculative and transcendental. Thus, being himself still a representative of Late Renaissance thought, he overcame its paradoxical and incoherent fusing of the irrational and the rational. He opened the way for the coming era of science in which the sovereign human spirit victoriously transcended all limits of rational investigation into the infinitely large and the infinitely small.

Notes

Notes to Introduction

1. A panorama of this kind, unequaled in artistic plasticity and lucidity was given by Jacob Burckhardt in his *Kultur der Renaissance in Italien*. Since the era of historism, research in the various special fields has been advanced so much that any attempt to draw a comprehensive picture is bound to fail. (The book of Dagobert Frey, *Gotik und Renaissance*, Augsburg, 1929, offers an example.) The task of the historian of our time is to keep strictly to the problems of his proper field, but to demonstrate them under the visual angle of the cultural totality of which they form a part.

2. First published in the *Historische Zeitschrift*, 1918 (volume 119). Republished in volume 1 of the posthumous edition of the scholar's writings, *Kunstgeschichte als Geistesgeschichte* (Munich, 1923).

3. Edited by Johannes Wilde and Karl M. Swoboda under the title *Geschichte der italienischen Kunst im Zeitalter der Renaissance*, 2 vols. (Munich, 1927-29).

Notes to Chapter I

1. The Nuremberg Chronicle of 1493, published by Albrecht Dürer's godfather, the printer and publisher Anton Koberger, illustrated by Michael Wolgemut and Hans Pleydenwurff, is a book of popular instruction and information.

2. The illustrations to Boccaccio's *De Claris Mulieribus*, published in 1473 by Johann Zainer in Ulm, offer characteristic examples.

3. The most comprehensive publication of Dürer's writings is to be found in K. Lange and F. Fuhse, *Dürer's schriftlicher Nachlass* (Halle, 1893), and W. M. Conway, *Literary Remains of Albrecht Dürer* (Cambridge, 1893).

4. Munich, Graphische Sammlung. W. L. Schreiber, *Handbuch der Holz- und Metallschnitte des 15. Jahrhunderts* (Leipzig, 1926-1930), no. 709.

5. Lionel Cust, *The Master E. S. and the "Ars Moriendi"* (Oxford, 1908), plate IV A.

6. Berlin, Kupferstichkabinett. *Zeichnungen von Albrecht Dürer in Nachbildungen*, by Friedrich Lippmann and Friedrich Winkler, 7 vols. (Berlin: G. Grote, 1883-1905, 1927-1929). Vols. 1-5 edited by F. Lippmann; vols. 6-7 edited by F. Winkler, no. 40. Hereafter cited as Lippmann. F. Winkler, *Die Zeichnungen Albrecht Dürers* (Berlin: 1936-1939), no. 559.

7. M. Dvořák, "Dürer's Apokalypse," *Kunstgeschichte als Geistesgeschichte*. E. Gothein, "Das Kreuzwunder," *Schriften zur Kulturgeschichte der Renaissance, Reformation und Gegenreformation* (Munich, 1924), vol. II, pp. 62 ff.

8. Vienna, Kunsthistorisches Museum. Lippmann, no. 423; Winkler, no. 944.

9. *Vnderweysung der messung mit dem zirkel und richtscheyt* (Nuremberg, 1525).

10. *Etliche vnderricht zu befestigung der Stett, Schlosz und Flecken* (Nuremberg, 1527).

11. *Hierin sind begriffen vier bücher von menschlicher Proportion . . .* (Nuremberg, 1528).

12. The manuscripts are preserved in the British Museum, London. Conway, *Literary Remains*, pp. 167 ff. See also Erwin Panofsky, *Dürers Kunsttheorie* (Berlin, 1915), and *Albrecht Dürer*, 2 vols. (Princeton, 1943), vol. I, chapter viii, "Dürer as a Theorist of Art."

13. P. Duhem, *Études sur Léonard de Vinci*, 3 vols. (Paris, 1906–13), 2. Sér. XI. "Nicolaus de Cues et Léonard de Vinci."

14. Lippmann, no. 586; Winkler, no. 19.

15. The Rayl Epitaph in St. Lorenz, Nuremberg, offers a good comparison.

16. J. Meder, *Dürer-Katalog* (Vienna: Gilhofer und Ranschburg, 1932), no. 227. Hereafter referred to as Meder.

17. *Der Ritter vom Turn* (Basel: Michael Furter, 1493). Meder, p. 273, VI.

18. *Das Narrenschyff* (Basel: Johann Bergmann von Olpe, 1494). Meder, p. 273, VII.

19. J. B. A. Lassus, *Album de Villard de Honnecourt* (Paris, 1858), planche 36.

20. Lwów, Lubomirski Museum. Lippmann, no. 613; Winkler, no. 27.

21. London, British Museum. Lippmann, no. 611; Winkler, no. 33.

22. Hamburg, Kunsthalle. Lippmann, no. 620; Winkler, no. 56.

23. Paris, Louvre. Lippmann, no. 624; Winkler, no. 85.

24. Oxford, Ashmolean Museum. Lippmann, no. 392; Winkler, no. 99.

25. Bremen, Kunsthalle. Lippmann, no. 109; Winkler, no. 96.

26. London, British Museum. Lippmann, no. 219; Winkler, no. 114.

27. W. Dilthey, "Der entwicklungsgeschichtliche Pantheismus nach seinem Zusammenhang mit den älteren pantheistischen Systemen," *Gesammelte Schriften*, vol. 2, p. 324.

28. Heinrich Wölfflin, *Die Bamberger Apokalypse* (Munich, 1921).

29. Nuremberg: Anton Koberger, 1491.

30. Munich, Staatsbibliothek, Cim. 58.

31. Heinrich Wölfflin, in *Die Kunst Albrecht Dürers* (Munich 1905), the basic representation of Dürer's art in the spirit of its form, brought a masterly analysis of the painting's formal values. — *Albrecht Dürer*, by E. Panofsky, is the most important work on Dürer since Wölfflin's book. It supplements the understanding of form, as advanced by Wölfflin, with the most comprehensive representation of iconography and ideological background.—H. Tietze and E. Tietze-Conrat made the attempt of a chronological and critical catalogue of Dürer's entire work. *Kritisches Verzeichnis der Werke Albrecht Dürers* (Augsburg and Basel, 1928–38).

32. The so-called Grosses Rasenstück (Large Piece of Turf), 1503. Vienna, Albertina. Lippmann, no. 472; Winkler, no. 346.

33. 1502. Vienna, Albertina. Lippmann, no. 468; Winkler, no. 248.

34. 1521. London, British Museum. Lippmann, no. 290; Winkler, no. 823.

35. Die Madonna mit den vielen Tieren. Pen and water-color drawing. 1503. Vienna, Albertina. Lippmann, no. 709; Winkler, no. 297.

36. K. Giehlow, *Kaiser Maximilians I. Gebetbuch* (Vienna, 1907).

37. Nos. 9961–62. Beatus page fol. 14.

38. The Small Woodcut Passion. Descent from the Cross (Adam von Bartsch, *Le Peintre graveur*, 21 vols., Vienne, 1803–21, no. 42; Meder, no. 151).

39. 1522. Metal point on green prepared paper. Bremen, Kunsthalle. Lippmann, no. 131; Winkler, no. 886.

40. 1520. Charcoal. Paris, Louvre. Lippmann, no. 361; Winkler, no. 805.

41. *Enchiridion Militis Christiani* (Antwerp: Th. Martinus, 1503; Basel: Froben, 1518).

Notes to Chapter II

1. The most clarifying explanation of the spiritual meaning of the Four Apostles (now in the Aeltere Pinakothek at Munich) was given by Ernst Heidrich, *Dürer und die Reformation* (Leipzig, 1909).

2. Compare for the following the basic work by Ernst Troeltsch, *Die Soziallehren der Christlichen Kirchen und Gruppen*, vol. I of *Gesammelte Schriften* (Tübingen, 1912).

3. The basic monograph on the master was written by H. A. Schmid, *Die Gemälde und Zeichnungen des Matthias Grünewald* (Strassburg i.E., 1911).

4. The documentary clarification of the Grünewald problem was achieved by W. K. Zülch, "Eine Grünewaldurkunde," *Jahresbericht der Oeffentlichen Kunstsammlung Basel*, Neue Folge, vol. 24 (1927), p. 40. See also his *Der historische Grünewald Mathis Gothardt-Neithardt* (Munich, 1938).

5. W. Vöge, *Niclas Hagnower, der Meister des Isenheimer Hochaltars und seine Frühwerke* (Freiburg i.Br., 1931).

6. Heinrich Feurstein, "Zur Deutung des Bildgehaltes bei Grünewald," *Beiträge zur Geschichte der deutschen Kunst, herausgegeben von Ernst Buchner und Karl Feuchtmayr*, vol. I (Augsburg, 1924), p. 137 ff.

7. H. Feurstein, *Matthias Grünewald* (Bonn, 1930), p. 130–131.

8. K. W. Zülch, *Der historische Grünewald*, p. 228.

9. M. J. Friedländer, *Die Zeichnungen von Matthias Grünewald* (Berlin, 1927).

10. G. Schoenberger, "Grünewalds Zeichnungen zum Isenheimer Altar," *Beiträge zur Geschichte der deutschen Kunst*, I, 164 ff.

11. Joachim von Sandrart, *Teutsche Academie der Edlen Bau-, Bild- und Mahlerey-Künste* (Nuremberg, 1675).

12. This was the case with the so-called "Töpferaltar" in the St. Stephan's Cathedral in Vienna, a beautiful work of Austrian terra-cotta sculpture of the early sixteenth century which represents the Holy Trinity in the shape of three male figures. (A. Feulner, *Deutsche Plastik des 16. Jahrhunderts*, Munich, 1926, pl. 36.) It had to be removed in the eighteenth century from the cathedral to the little church of St. Helena near Baden because it was offensive to the current dogma. This had not been the case in the fifteenth century where such repre-

sentations more frequently occur, e.g. in the Coronation of the Holy Virgin by Holbein the Elder in The Basilica of S. Maria Maggiore, 1499. Still earlier in the century we find an even stranger representation of the Trinity in the shape of three heads grown together, having four eyes in common. The Trinity appears thus in a German Genesis of the fifteenth century in the Pierpont Morgan Library, New York (M. 268, p. 1 verso and p. 2 recto). Furthermore, the Trinity appears thus in a panel in the Monastery Neustift near Brixen, a work of the Tyrolian Master of the Augustinus Altar about 1460; it represents the church father celebrating mass and pondering over the secret of the Trinity. These may be remains of the mystical fourteenth century, yet they anticipate Grünewald's concept in an illuminating way.

13. Basel, Oeffentliche Kunstsammlung. H. Koegler, *Die Basler Handzeichnungen des Urs Graf* (1926), no. 88.

14. Eisenmann, no. 145, in his article in Julius Meyer's *Künstlerlexikon* (Leipzig, 1872), vol. II. It is a free copy after Cranach's engraving of 1520 and was used as book-illustration in *Acta et res gestae Dr. Martini Lutheri* (Strassburg: Johann Schott, 1521).

15. A most valuable source book to the history of those religious extremists is *Gottfried Arnolds Unpartheyische Kirchen- und Ketzer-Historie, Vom Anfang des Neuen Testaments Biss auf das Jahr Christi 1688* (Franckfurt am Mayn, 1729).

16. E. Buchner, *Albrecht Altdorfer und sein Kreis. Gedächtnisausstellung zum 400. Todesjahr Altdorfers* (München 1938); *Amtlicher Katalog*, no. 34; O. Benesch, *Der Maler Albrecht Altdorfer* (Vienna, 1938), pp. 21–22.

17. The woodcut by Michael Ostendorfer (J. D. Passavant, *Le Peintre Graveur*, 6 vols. (Leipzig, 1860–64), no. 13) is preserved in the Print Room of the Veste Coburg. Lange-Fuhse, *Dürers schriftlicher Nachlass* (Halle, 1893), p. 381; see also Catalogue of the Munich Exhibition 1938, no. 710.

18. E. Bloch, *Thomas Münzer als Theologe der Revolution* (Munich, 1921).

19. B. Kurth, "Ein unbekanntes Jugendwerk J. Ratgebs," *Beiträge zur Geschichte der oberdeutschen Kunst*, vol. 1, pp. 186 ff.; G. Schoenberger, "J. Ratgeb," *Städel-Jahrbuch*, vol. 5 (Frankfurt, 1926), p. 55 ff.; O. Benesch, "Zum Werk J. Ratgebs," *Zeitschrift für Bildende Kunst*, vol. 61 (1927–28), pp. 49 ff.

Notes to Chapter III

1. *Studies in the History of Science*, edited by Charles Singer (Oxford, 1917 and 1921); A. Castiglioni, *Storia della Medicina* (Milano, 1936).

2. A. C. Klebs in *Papers of the Bibliographical Society of America* (Chicago), XI (1917), 75; XII (1918), 41. The most beautiful fifteenth-century herbal is the *Hortus Sanitatis*, published in 1492 by Stefan Arndes in Lübeck.

3. Carolus Bovillus, *Liber de intellectu; Liber de sensu; Liber de nihilo; Ars oppositorum; Liber de generatione; Liber de sapiente*, etc. (Parisiis: ex officina H. Stephani, 1570), and *Physicorum elementorum libri decem* (Impressa Parrhisiis: in aedibus Ascensianis, 1512); E. Cassirer, *Individuum und Kosmos in der Philosophie der Renaissance* (Leipzig, 1927), pp. 93 ff. (*Studien der Bibliothek Warburg*, vol. X). (The *Liber de sapiente* is reprinted in the same volume, pp. 299 ff.)

4. O. Benesch, "Der Zwettler Altar und die Anfänge Jörg Breus," *Beiträge zur Geschichte der deutschen Kunst*, vol. II (Augsburg, 1928).

5. O. Benesch, *Katalog der Stiftlichen Kunstsammlungen Klosterneuburg*, vol. I, nos. 81–84; O. Fischer, *Die altdeutsche Malerei in Salzburg* (Leipzig, 1908), pp. 118 ff.

6. O. Benesch, "Der Zwettler Altar und die Anfänge Jörg Breus."

7. O. Benesch, "Die Anfänge Lucas Cranachs," *Jahrbuch der Kunsthistorischen Sammlungen*, Neue Folge, vol. II (Vienna, 1928).

8. W. Windelband, *Lehrbuch der Geschichte der Philosophie* (Tübingen, 1935), ch. IV. "Philosophie der Renaissance," § 29, "Makrokosmos und Mikrokosmos."

9. M. J. Friedländer, *Albrecht Altdorfer, der Maler von Regensburg* (Leipzig, 1891), and *Albrecht Altdorfer* (Berlin, 1923); H. Tietze, *Albrecht Altdorfer* (Leipzig, 1923); O. Benesch, *Der Maler Albrecht Altdorfer* (Vienna, 1939); L. Baldass, *Albrecht Altdorfer* (Zurich, 1941).

10. T. Sturge Moore, A. Altdorfer, A book of 71 woodcuts (Little Engravings classical and contemporary, Nr. 1), London 1902, pl. 3.

11. Paris, Louvre. Hanna L. Becker, *Die Handzeichnungen Albrecht Altdorfers* (Munich, 1938), no. 56.

12. The Satyr's Family, Bartsch, no. 69; Meder, no. 65. It seems that the ensemble of fabulous beings enacting the forest legend in Altdorfer's picture is the same as in Dürer's engraving Hercules (Bartsch, no. 73; Meder, no. 63).

13. Dated 1510. Berlin, Deutsches Museum.

14. J. Meder, "A. Altdorfers Donaureise in 1511," *Mitteilungen der Gesellschaft für vervielfältigende Kunst* (Vienna, 1902).

15. M. Weinberger, *Wolf Huber* (Leipzig, 1930).

16. P. Halm, "Die Landschaftszeichnungen des Wolf Huber," *Münchner Jahrbuch der bildenden Kunst*, Neue Folge, vol. VII (1930).

17. O. Benesch, "Erhard Altdorfer als Maler," *Jahrbuch der preussischen Kunstsammlungen*, vol. 37 (1936), pp. 157 ff.

18. J. Meder, *Handzeichnungen alter Meister aus der Albertina*, Neue Folge (Vienna, 1922), vol. I, pl. 30.

19. Basel, Oeffentliche Kunstsammlung. P. Ganz, *Handzeichnungen Schweizerischer Meister des XV.–XVIII. Jahrhunderts* (Basel, 1904–1908), vol. I, pl. 21.

20. *Dess Buchs Meteorum Caput I.*

21. London, British Museum. Halm, "Die Landschaftzeichnungen des Wolf Huber," fig. 41.

22. London, University College. K. T. Parker, *Belvedere*, VIII, 78 ff.

23. Bartsch, no. 67; W. Schmidt, no. 103, in his article in Julius Meyer's *Künstlerlexikon* (Leipzig, 1872), vol. I. H. Voss, *Albrecht Altdorfer und Wolf Huber* (Leipzig, 1910), pl. 32 (*Meister der Graphik*, vol. 3).

24. W. Dilthey, "Auffassung und Analyse des Menschen im 15. und 16. Jahrhundert," *Gesammelte Schriften*, vol. 2, pp. 80 ff.

Notes to Chapter IV

1. Konrad Burdach, *Reformation Renaissance Humanismus* (Berlin, 1928).

2. *Opera Hrosvite illustris virginis et monialis germane gente Saxonica orte nuper a Conrado Celte inventa* (Nuremberg, 1501); *Quatuor Libri Amorum* (Nuremberg, 1502).

3. H. A. Schmid, *Forschungen über Hans Burgkmair*, Dissertation (Munich, 1888), p. 32; E. Panofsky, "Conrad Celtes und Kunz von der Rosen," *Art Bulletin*, vol. 24 (1942), p. 42; A. Burkhard, *Hans Burgkmair der Aeltere* (*Meister der Graphik*, vol. 15), (Berlin, 1932), catalogue no. 9, dated 1507; M. Geisberg, *Der deutsche Einblatt-Holzschnitt* (München, 1923–29), no. 504.

4. Karlsruhe, Kunsthalle. A. Burkhard, *Hans Burgkmair d.Ae.*, (Leipzig, s.a.), pp. 79, 80.

5. O. Reinhart Collection, Winterthur. H. Ankwicz v. Kleehoven, "Cranachs Bildnisse des Dr. Cuspinian und seiner Frau," *Jahrbuch der preussischen Kunstsammlungen*, vol. 48 (1927), pp. 230 ff.; M. J. Friedländer und J. Rosenberg, *Die Gemälde von Lucas Cranach* (Berlin: Deutscher Verein für Kunstwissenschaft, 1932), nos. 6 and 7.

6. Count Wilczek, Castle Kreuzenstein near Vienna.

7. Nuremberg, Germanisches Museum. Friedländer-Rosenberg, nos. 8, 9.

8. Berlin, Deutsches Museum.

9. Formerly Monastery of Herzogenburg, Lower Austria. E. Buchner, "Die Augsburger Tafelmalerei der Spätgotik," *Beiträge zur Geschichte der deutschen Kunst*, vol. II (Augsburg, 1928), pp. 81 ff.

10. Vienna, Kunsthistorisches Museum. Inv. no. 1405. J. Wilde, *Jahrbuch der Kunsthistorischen Sammlungen*, N.F., vol. 13 (1939).

11. Florence, Uffizi. Friedländer-Rosenberg, no. 342.

12. Nuremberg, Freiherr von Scheurl Collection. Friedländer-Rosenberg, no. 22.

13. J. C. Schuchardt. *L. Cranach der Aeltere, Leben und Werke* (Leipzig, 1851, 1871); J. Heller, *Lucas Cranach's Leben und Werke* (Nuremberg, 1854); E. Flechsig, *Cranachstudien* (Leipzig, 1900).

14. Bartsch, no. 116; Schuchardt, no. 123.

15. Schuchardt, no. 3.

16. Leopold von Ranke, *Deutsche Geschichte im Zeitalter der Reformation* (Berlin, 1839–47).

17. Dated 1524. Bartsch, no. 104; Meder, no. 102.

18. Bartsch, no. 77; Schuchardt, no. 97.

19. The Wittenberg relic-book (Heiligthumsbuch) illustrated with woodcuts by Cranach, representing the sacred objects, was published in 1509. C. Dodgson, *Catalogue of Early German and Flemish Woodcuts* (London, British Museum, 1911), vol. II, pp. 290 ff.

20. Bartsch, no. 5; Schuchardt, no. 6.

21. Leipzig, Museum der bildenden Künste. Friedländer-Rosenberg, no. 125.

22. Schuchardt, no. 179.

23. Formerly Berlin, Baroness R. von Goldschmidt-Rothschild Collection. Friedländer-Rosenberg, no. 160.

24. Friedländer-Rosenberg, nos. 253, 254.

25. O. Benesch, *Mitteilungen der Gesellschaft für vervielfältigende Kunst* (Vienna, 1932), p. 14.

26. Dresden, Gemäldegalerie. Friedländer-Rosenberg, nos. 53, 54.

27. Dresden, Gemäldegalerie. Friedländer-Rosenberg, no. 286.

28. Friedländer-Rosenberg, no. 49.

29. Brussels, Musée des Beaux-Arts. Friedländer-Rosenberg, no. 266.

30. W. Dilthey, "Das natürliche System der Geisteswissenschaften im 17. Jahrhundert," IV: "Melanchthon und die erste Ausbildung des natürlichen Systems in Deutschland," *Gesammelte Schriften*, vol. 2.

31. Bartsch, no. 105; Meder, no. 104.

32. F. Lippmann, *Lucas Cranach: Sammlung von Nachbildungen seiner vorzüglichsten Holzschnitte und seiner Stiche* (Berlin, 1895), pl. 55. Woodcut by Lucas Cranach the Younger after a painting by his father.

33. The basic work for all research on Holbein is the fundamental article "Hans Holbein d.J." by H. A. Schmid in Thieme-Becker, *Allgemeines Lexikon der Bildenden Künstler*, vol. 13 (Leipzig, 1924). See also A. Woltmann, *Holbein und seine Zeit* (Leipzig, 1866 and 1868); A. B. Chamberlain, *Hans Holbein the Younger* (London, 1913).

34. Paul Ganz, *Die Handzeichnungen Hans Holbeins d.J.*, Kritischer Katalog (Berlin, 1937). All existing drawings by Holbein were published in facsimile by the Swiss scholar (*Denkmäler deutscher Kunst, herausgegeben vom Deutschen Verein für Kunstwissenschaft*). The drawings for Erasmus' hands in the portrait of Longford Castle are in the Louvre. Ganz, nos. 6 and 7.

35. J. Huizinga, *Erasmus* (Basel, 1928); B. de Ligt, *Erasmus begrepen uit de Geest der Renaissance* (Arnhem, 1936).

36. *Erasmus Desiderius Encomium moriae i.e. Stultitiae Laus, Lob der torheit. Basler Ausgabe von 1515, mit den Randzeichnungen von Hans Holbein d.J., in Facsimile mit einer Einführung herausgegeben von H. A. Schmid* (Basel, 1931).

37. Basel, Oeffentliche Kunstsammlung. E. Schilling, *Zeichnungen der Künstlerfamilie Holbein* (Frankfurt, 1937), pl. 17.

38. Basel, Oeffentliche Kunstsammlung.

39. Darmstadt, Schloss.

40. H. A. Schmid, "Holbeins Tätigkeit für die Basler Verleger," *Jahrbuch der preussischen Kunstsammlungen*, vol. 20 (1899).

41. William Roper, *The Life and Death of Sir Thomas More* (Paris, 1626; Oxford, 1716), is the most important contemporary source on the scholar.

42. Basel, Oeffentliche Kunstsammlung. Ganz, no. 24. O. Pächt has demonstrated that the inscriptions of the names in this drawing were probably made by Nicholas Kratzer, who taught astronomy to More's children ("Holbein and Kratzer as Collaborators," *Burlington Magazine*, June 1944).

43. Ganz, no. 30. For the drawings at Windsor Castle see also K. T. Parker, *The Drawings of Holbein at Windsor Castle* (London: Oxford, 1945).

44. Ganz, no. 31.

45. Ganz, no. 27.

46. Windsor Castle. Ganz, no. 58.

47. Windsor Castle. Ganz, no. 35.

48. Windsor Castle. Ganz, no. 19. Study for the Portrait of 1527 in Lambeth Palace, London.

49. Dated 1528. Paris, Louvre.

50. "Meyster Hans holbein der maller spricht, man muss im den disch bass uszlegen, ob er gang." E. His, "Holbeins Verhältnis zur Basler Reformation," *Repertorium für Kunstwissenschaft*, vol. II (1879), p. 156.

51. R. Pfeiffer, "Humanitas Erasmiana," *Studien der Bibliothek Warburg*, vol. XXII (Leipzig, 1931).

Notes to Chapter V

1. M. Dvořák, "Ueber die geschichtlichen Voraussetzungen des niederländischen Romanismus," *Kunstgeschichte als Geistesgeschichte*, p. 208.

2. Dated 1506. Berlin, Deutsches Museum.

3. Berlin, Kaiser Friedrich Museum. For all of the works by Flemish and Dutch artists discussed in these chapters see M. J. Friedländer, *Die altniederländische Malerei*, 14 vols. (Berlin-Leiden, 1924–1937).

4. L. Baldass, "Gotik und Renaissance im Werk des Quinten Metsys," *Jahrbuch der Kunsthistorischen Sammlungen*, Neue Folge, vol. 7 (Vienna, 1933).

5. Chatsworth, Collection of the Duke of Devonshire.

6. C. Justi, "Juan de Flandes," *Jahrbuch der preussischen Kunstsammlungen*, vol. VIII (1887).

7. See the publication *Hortulus Animae* by F. Dörnhöffer (Frankfurt, 1907).

8. G. Glück, "Bildnisse von Juan de Flandes," *Pantheon*, vol. 8 (1931), pp. 313 ff.

9. It is superior in quality to another version of the same portrait in the Baron Thyssen Collection, Schloss Rohoncz. *Exhibition Neue Pinakothek* (Munich, 1930), cat. no. 166 (attribution by M. J. Friedländer). Court portraits of this type were frequently repeated for gift purposes, often by the masters themselves. The quality of the painting proves it as the original version which served as a model for the other.

10. Friedländer, *Altniederländische Malerei*, vol. IX.

11. Friedländer, *Altniederländische Malerei*, vol. VII, p. 10.

12. Carel van Mander, *Le Livre des Peintres*, ed. H. Hymans (Paris, 1884), I, 264.

13. The so-called "Hermaphrodite," Venice, Academy.

14. F. Winkler, *Die flämische Buchmalerei des 15. und 16. Jahrhunderts* (Leipzig, 1925), p. 150.

15. *Beschreibender Katalog der Handzeichnungen in der Graphischen Sammlung Albertina,* ed. Alfred Stix, 5 vols. (Vienna: A. Schroll, 1926–1933), vol. II, O. Benesch, *Die Zeichnungen der niederländischen Schulen des 15. und 16. Jahrhunderts* (Vienna, 1928), no. 35.

16. Friedländer, *Altniederländische Malerei*, vol. XI.

17. L. Baldass, "Die niederländischen Maler des spätgotischen Stiles," *Jahrbuch der Kunsthistorischen Sammlungen*, Neue Folge, vol. XI (Vienna, 1937).

18. W. Friedländer, "Die Entstehung des antiklassischen Stils," *Repertorium für Kunstwissenschaft*, vol. 46 (1925).

19. Berlin, Kaiser Friedrich Museum.

20. Richmond, Sir Herbert Cook Collection.

21. *Beschreibender Katalog*, vol. II, no. 36.

22. Munich, Von Bissing Collection. Friedländer, *Altniederländische Malerei*, vol. XI.

23. Vienna, Liechtenstein Gallery.

24. Formerly in the Figdor Collection, Vienna.

25. J. Huizinga, *The Waning of the Middle Ages* (London, 1937), p. 179.

Notes to Chapter VI

1. The most magnificent sets of those tapestries are preserved in the Kunsthistorisches Museum in Vienna and the Royal Castle at Madrid. See *Die Wiener Gobelinsammlung*, ed. by L. Baldass (Vienna, 1920–).

2. M. Dvořák, "Ueber die geschichtlichen Voraussetzungen des niederländischen Romanismus," *Kunstgeschichte als Geistesgeschichte*. See also O. Benesch, introduction to *Beschreibender Katalog der Handzeichnungen in der Graphischen Sammlung Albertina*, vol. II, *Die Zeichnungen der niederländischen Schulen des XV. und XVI. Jahrhunderts*. Wien 1928.

3. The Last Judgment from the Town Hall of Diest (now in the Museum of Brussels) is an example of the Bosch style before Bosch, deriving from the tradition of the international style.

4. R. van Bastelaer, *Les Estampes de Pieter Bruegel l'Ancien* (Bruxelles, 1908), no. 123.

5. Drawing in the Albertina. *Beschreibender Katalog*, vol. II, no. 79.

6. K. Tolnai, *Die Zeichnungen Pieter Bruegels* (Munich, 1925).

7. R. van Bastelaer, *Pieter Bruegel l'Ancien, Son Oeuvre et Son Temps* (Bruxelles, 1907); M. J. Friedländer, *Von Eyck bis Bruegel* (Berlin, 1916), p. 160, and *Die altniederländische Malerei*, vol. XIV (Leiden, 1937); Axel Romdahl, "Pieter Bruegel der Aeltere und sein Kunstschaffen," *Jahrbuch der Kunsthistorischen Sammlungen des Allerhöchsten Kaiserhauses*, vol. XXV.

8. Albertina, *Beschreibender Katalog*, vol. II, no. 81.

9. Gustav Glück, *Bruegels Gemälde* (Vienna, 1932).

10. G. Glück, following Carel van Mander, has first drawn attention to a Dutch precursor of Bruegel, Jan van Amstel, the so-called Braunschweiger Monogrammist, who several years before Bruegel came to similar solutions — to represent biblical events (The Feeding of the Five Thousand, The Carrying

of the Cross) as naturalistic mass scenes (*Pieter Bruegels Gemälde im Kunst-historischen Hofmuseum zu Wien*, Brussels, 1910). Jan van Amstel, indeed, had a decisive influence on Bruegel, yet his mode is as modern as that of Bruegel and shows closer connection with the leading Dutch Renaissance masters (Lucas van Leyden, Jan van Scorel, and their followers) than with any traditional by-current.

11. Drawing in the Albertina, *Beschreibender Katalog*, vol. II, no. 76.

12. W. Fraenger, *Der Bauern-Bruegel und das deutsche Sprichwort* (Erlenbach-Zürich, 1923).

13. Charles de Tolnay, *Pierre Bruegel l'Ancien* (Bruxelles, 1935), p. 18.

14. The Adoration of the Magi. Bartsch, no. 6.

15. "Pieter Bruegel der Aeltere," *Kunstgeschichte als Geistesgeschichte*.

16. It is the great merit of Charles de Tolnay's publications to have demonstrated the close linkage of Bruegel's art with the philosophical and religious framework of the Northern Renaissance. *Bruegels Handzeichnungen* (Munich, 1925); *Pierre Bruegel l'Ancien* (Bruxelles, 1935); "Studien zu den Gemälden Pieter Bruegels d.Ae.," *Jahrbuch der Kunsthistorischen Sammlungen*, Neue Folge, vol. 8 (Vienna, 1934).

17. W. Dilthey, *Weltanschauung und Analyse des Menschen* (*Gesammelte Schriften*, vol. 2), "Auffassung und Analyse des Menschen," p. 85.

18. La Bataille de Karesme et de Charnage. J. Huizinga, *The Waning of the Middle Ages* (London, 1937), p. 193.

19. This interpretation was first suggested by de Tolnay. It is proved by a poem of Jacob Cats ("Silenus Alcibiadis," 1617), illustrated by A. van de Venne. See O. Benesch, *Artistic and Intellectual Trends from Rubens to Daumier as shown in Book-Illustration* (Cambridge: Harvard College Library, 1943), p. 38.

20. See W. Fraenger, *Der Bauern-Bruegel*.

21. A. E. Popham, "P. Bruegel and Abraham Ortelius," *Burlington Magazine*, vol. 59 (1931), pp. 184 ff.

22. G. Glück, "Peter Bruegel the Elder and Classical Antiquity," *Art Quarterly*, (1943), pp. 167 ff.

23. Another version of the painting exists in the J. Herbrand Collection, Paris. Glück considers it as the original because the figure of the flying Daedalus, missing in the Brussels painting, appears here in the upper center. The shepherd turns his look upwards to him, an attitude which finds no explanation in the Brussels painting.

24. We are reminded of a paragraph by Giordano Bruno: "Although some celestial bodies shine with their own light and are warm, however, the sun does not shine for the sun, and the earth not for the same earth, and water not for the same water; every star rather receives its light from an opposite one, as we see from elevated points, for instance from mountains, the entire sea shining, whereas, on the sea itself, we see this reflected light only to the extent of the image of the sun or the moon opposite."

"Sesto, come di corpi, benché altri sieno per sé lucidi e caldi, non per questo il sole luce il sole e la terra luce alla medesima terra ed acqua alla medesima acqua; ma sempre il lume procede dall'apposito astro, come sensibilmente veggiamo tutto il mar lucente da luoghi eminenti, come da monti; ed essendo noi nel mare, e quando siamo ne l'istesso campo, non veggiamo risplendere se non quanto a certa poca dimensione il lume del sole e della luna ne si oppone." *De l'infinito, universo e mondi* (Venice, 1584), Proemiale Epistola. Abstract of the third dialogue, paragraph 6.

25. E. Mâle, *L'Art religieux de la fin du moyen age en France* (Paris, 1908), "La vie, le vice et la vertu," pp. 316 ff.

26. A. Mongan and P. J. Sachs, *Drawings in the Fogg Museum of Art* (Cambridge: Harvard University Press, 1940), no. 459.

27. A collector, Nicolas Jonghelinck, is mentioned in documents as the owner of the cycle in 1565. G. Glück, *Bruegels Gemälde* (Vienna, 1932), p. 52.

28. *Instauratarum scientiarum per F. Thomam Campanellam juxta propria dogmata, ex natura et scriptura Dei Codicibus Tomi X. III. De sensu Rerum et Magia.*

29. *De l'infinito, universo e mondi.*

30. *De gli eroici furori* (Paris, 1585). Prima Parte. Dialogo primo. "Questo capitano e la voluntade umana, che siede in poppa de l'anima, con un picciol temone de la raggione governando gli affetti d'alcune potenze interiori contra l'onde degli empiti naturali."

Notes to Chapter VII

1. We owe the most extensive and important research on the School of Fontainebleau to L. Dimier. See *Le Primatice, peintre, sculpteur et architecte des rois de France* (Paris, 1900); *French Painting in the Sixteenth Century* (London, 1904); "Les Origines de l'Art Français," *Les Arts* (Paris, 1905); *Fontainebleau* (Paris, 1925); *Histoire de la Peinture Française des Origines au Retour de Vouet, 1300 à 1627* (Paris, 1925).

2. K. Kusenberg, *Le Rosso* (Paris, 1931).

3. W. Friedländer, "Die Entstehung des antiklassischen Stils," *Repertorium für Kunstwissenschaft*, vol. 46 (1925).

4. The basic definition of Mannerism as a great chapter of the history of ideas was given by Max Dvořák, "Ueber Greco und den Manierismus," *Kunstgeschichte als Geistesgeschichte*.

5. See Chapter VI, note 1.

6. P. Lavallée, *Le Dessin Français du XIIIe au XVIe Siècle* (Paris, 1930), p. 92.

7. M. Crick-Kuntziger, "L'auteur des cartons de 'Vertumne et Pomone'," *Oud Holland*, vol. 44 (1927), pp. 159 ff.

8. Épigrammes à l'imitation de Martial, livre V, no. 18.

9. *Marguerites de la Marguerite des Princesses, Tres illustre Royne de Navarre. A Lyon, par Jean de Tournes 1547*. Our reproductions, nos. 63 and 64, are taken from the volumes of the Frances Hofer Collection, deposited with the Houghton Library, Harvard University. We are indebted to Mr. and Mrs. Philip Hofer for the permission of reproduction.

10. "Les Vers d'Eurymedon et de Calliree: Le Baing de Calliree."

11. M. L. Gothein, *History of Garden Art* (London, 1928), I, 400.

12. Ovid, *Metamorphoses* (Lyon: Jean de Tournes, French edition, 1557), p. 136, "Ciparisse en Cipre."

13. This woodcut is added to an Italian treatise by Gabriel Symeon on the nature of the moon and the names given to the Goddess Diana by classical authors. *La Natura et Effetti della Luna nelle cose humane, passando per i XII Segni del Cielo, Insieme co i nomi che gl'Autori Greci & Latini hanno attribuiti a Diana. La Fontana di Roiag in Overnia* (1558). See Chapter VII, note 9.

14. O. Benesch, "Jean Cousin fils dessinateur," *Prométhée*, I, (Paris, 1939), 271 ff.

15. *The Renaissance* (1873).

16. A. P. F. Robert-Dumesnil, *Le Peintre-graveur français*, 11 vols. (Paris, 1835), vol. 5, nos. 54–59.

17. Robert-Dumesnil, nos. 27–49.

18. J. Babelon, *Germain Pilon* (Paris, 1927).

19. Flavinio de Birague wrote an eulogy on the little animal.

Épitaphe d'un petit chien de Madame la chancelière de Birague

"Ce petit chien aima tellement sa maistresse,
Qu'après qu'elle eut quitté la terre pour les cieux,
Le regret causa tant en son cœur de tristesse,
Qu'après trois jours laissa le vivre soucieux."

Babelon, p. 67.

20. The terra-cotta model for the marble sculpture in St. Paul, in original size, is preserved in the Louvre. Pilon received the marble block for the sculpture, an order of Catherine de Medici, on April 4, 1586. Babelon, p. 68.

21. A highly important one of these drawings passed, unrecognized, in 1924 through a sale in Paris. *Dessins anciens*, Collection de M. X***. Hotel Drouot, Vendredi 11 Avril 1924, No. 37, "Hendrik Goltzius, La chasse au cerf." It was of considerable size (405:500 mm) and represented a stag hunt in the style of the courtly tapestries. Rich washes, which anticipated much of the technique of Callot, lent a magic chiaroscuro effect to it. May this brief aviso help trace the beautiful piece again.

22. The inner affinity of Bellange's art to the mystical trend in the thought of St. François de Sales was pointed out by Dvořák, "Ueber Greco," p. 272. St. François' religious thought had also a rational aspect which found its parallels in the works of Bellange's follower Jacques Callot. See O. Benesch, *Artistic and Intellectual Trends from Rubens to Daumier* (Harvard College Library, 1943), p. 20.

23. Etching, Robert-Dumesnil, vol. 5, no. 9.

24. Robert-Dumesnil, no. 7.

Notes to Chapter VIII

1. See O. Benesch, introduction to the chapter "Manierismus" in *Beschreibender Katalog der Handzeichnungen in der Graphischen Sammlung Albertina*, vol. IV, *Die Zeichnungen der deutschen Schulen* (Vienna, 1933).

2. *Nicolai Copernici Torinensis De Revolutionibus Orbium Coelestium Libri VI.* Norimbergae apud Joh. Petreium, Anno M.D. XLIII.

3. Liber I, "De ordine coelestium orbium," fol. 9 verso: "In medio vero omnium residet Sol. Quis enim in hoc pulcherrimo templo lampadem hanc in alio vel meliori loco poneret, quam unde totum simul possit illuminare? Siquidem non inepte quidam lucernam mundi, alii mentem, alii rectorem vocant. Trimegistus visibilem Deum, Sophoclis Electra intuentem omnia. Ita profecto tamquam in solio regali Sol residens circum agentem gubernat Astrorum familiam." (The translation of the Latin text is taken from Abraham Wolf, *A History of Science, Technology, and Philosophy in the 16th & 17th Centuries* (London, 1935), p. 16.)

4. Albertina, *Beschreibender Katalog*, vol. IV, no. 615.

5. Venice, Ducal Palace. See Charles de Tolnay, *Jerôme Bosch* (Bâle, 1937), pl. 28.

6. Van Beuningen Collection, Rotterdam. Ch. de Tolnay, "La Seconde Tour de Babel de Pierre Bruegel l'Ancien," *Annuaire des Musées Royaux des Beaux-Arts de Belgique* (1938), pp. 113 ff.

7. The "loxodrome," the course of a ship which cuts the meridians at a constant angle, was considered to be a circle. This led to errors in the drawing of charts which transform the spatial relation into planographic projection. The Portuguese Nunez discovered that it is actually a *spiral*, a discovery which furthered the improvement of charts. (T. H. Pledge, *Science since 1500*, London, 1939, p. 35.)

8. See O. Benesch, introduction to *Beschreibender Katalog der Handzeichnungen in der Graphischen Sammlung Albertina*, vol. II, *Die Zeichnungen der Niederländischen Schulen des XV. und XVI. Jahrhunderts* (Vienna, 1928).

9. See Chapter VI, note 24.

10. *La cena de le ceneri* (1584). Dialogo primo. "Conoscemo, che non é ch'un cielo, un'eterea reggione immensa, dove questi magnifici lumi serbano le proprie distanze, per commodità de la partecipazione de la perpetua vita. Questi fiammeggianti corpi son que'ambasciatori, che annunziano l'eccelenza de la gloria e maestà di Dio."

11. *De l'infinito, universo e mondi*. Dialogo primo. "Però, per la raggione de innumerabili gradi de perfezione, che denno esplicare la eccellenza divina incorporea per modo corporeo, denno essere innumerabili individui, che son questi grandi animali (de quali uno e questa terra, diva madre che ne ha parturiti ed alimenta e che oltre non ne riprendera), per la continenza di questi innumerabili si richiede un spacio infinito."

12. For the meaning of Tintoretto's composition as a mirror of the celestial universe see the essay by Charles de Tolnay, "The Music of the Universe," *Journal of the Walters Art Gallery*, VI (1943), 95, who arrived independently at the same results.

13. On Tintoretto, see M. Dvořák, *Geschichte der italienischen Kunst*, 2 vols. (Munich, 1927-29), II, 144 ff.

14. The author first expounded the relation of Tintoretto's art to scientific concepts and contemporary music in a lecture on "Titian and Tintoretto," delivered at the University of Cambridge in November 1939.

For the interrelation between cosmic speculation, musical and pictorial composition in Late Mannerism, see O. Benesch, *Artistic and Intellectual Trends* from *Rubens to Daumier* (Harvard College Library, 1943), pp. 29–30 (Lectures delivered in the Houghton Library, Harvard University, in March and April 1942). See also Ch. de Tolnay, "The Music of the Universe," *Journal of the Walters Art Gallery*, VI (1943), 101.

15. Eduard Lowinsky, *Das Antwerpener Motettenbuch Orlando di Lasso's und seine Beziehungen zum Motettenschaffen der niederländischen Zeitgenossen* (The Hague, 1937).

16. R. Hedicke, *Cornelis Floris und die Floris-Dekoration* (Berlin, 1913).

17. A splendid example is the design of a dedicatory thesis for Emperor Maximilian II, 1571. The original drawing is preserved in the Albertina. *Beschreibender Katalog*, vol. IV, no. 502.

18. *Tychonis Brahe Dani de Mundi Aetherei Recentioribus Phaenomenis Liber Secundus qui est de illustri stella caudata ab elapso fere triente Novembris Anni 1577, usq; in finem Januarij sequentis conspecta.* Uraniburgi, In Insula Hellesponti Danici Hvenna imprimebat Authoris Typographus Christophorus Vveida. Anno Domini MCLXXXVIII.

Page 189: "Nova Mundani Systematis Hypotyposis ab Authore nuper adinventa, quo tum vetus ille Ptolemaica redundantia & inconcinnitas, tum etiam recens Coperniana in motu Terrae Physica absurditas, excluduntur, omniaque Apparentiis Coelestibus aptissime correspondent."

19. Among the organ works of a late Manneristic Venetian composer we find one entitled "La Serpentina" (*Canzoni de intavolatura d'organo fatte alla francese di Vincenzo Pellegrini ecc.* In Venetia, Appresso Giacomo Vincenti, M.D.LXXXXIX). The musical design follows there a formal idea which plays such a great part in the compositional design of the Manneristic painters.

20. Paris, Louvre, Archives photographiques, no. 4442.

21. Museum of Braunschweig. *Zeichnungen Alter Meister im Landesmuseum zu Braunschweig* (Prestel-Gesellschaft), pl. 55.

22. Albertina, *Beschreibender Katalog*, vol. II, no. 283.

23. Veste Coburg, Print Room. Th. Muchall-Viebrook, *Deutsche Barockzeichnungen* (Munich), pl. 1.

24. Drawing in the Albertina. *Beschreibender Katalog*, vol. IV, no. 441. Executed as painting for the Wilhelmsfeste in 1597. See H. Peltzer, "Der Hofmaler H. von Aachen," *Jahrbuch der Kunsthistorischen Sammlungen*, vol. 30 (Vienna).

25. O. Hirschmann, "Carel van Manders Haarlemer Akademie," *Monatshefte für Kunstwissenschaft*, vol. 11 (1918), pp. 213 ff.

26. K. T. Parker, *Catalogue of the Collection of Drawings in the Ashmolean Museum* (Oxford, 1938), vol. I, no. 34.

27. O. Hirschmann, *Hendrik Goltzius* (Leipzig, 1919), *Meister der Graphik*, vol. 7.

28. C. M. A. A. Lindeman, *Joachim Anthonisz Wtewael* (Utrecht, 1929).

29. Dated 1593. A similar painting of the same subject is in the Staedel Institute, Frankfurt a.M.

30. Berlin, Kupferstichkabinett. J. Q. van Regteren-Altena, *Jacques de Gheyn, an Introduction to the Study of His Drawings* (Amsterdam, 1935), pl. 10.

31. *Tychonis Brahe Astronomiae instauratae Mechanica.* Noribergae, apud Levinum Hulsium. Anno M.DCII.

32. E. F. Appelt, J. *Kepplers astronomische Weltansicht* (Leipzig, 1849); Rudolf Wolf, *Geschichte der Astronomie* (München, 1877), pp. 281 ff.; Christoph Sigwart, *Kleine Schriften* (Tübingen, 1881), I, 182 ff.

33. Compare for the following the basic representation by Ernst Cassirer, *Das Erkenntnisproblem* (Berlin, 1906), I, 253 ff.

34. *Ioannis Keppleri Harmonices Mundi Libri V.* Lincii Austriae, Sumptibus Godofredi Tampachii Bibl. Francof. Excudebat Ioannes Plancus. Anno M.DC.XIX. The appendix deals with the harmonic theories of Ptolemy and Robert Flud.

35. *Mysterium Cosmographicum de Admirabili Proportione orbium coelestium. Libellus primus.* Tübingae in lucem datus Anno Christi M.DXCVI.

36. It is the old problem with which in the second half of the fifteenth century Piero della Francesca dealt ("Libellus de quinque corporibus regularibus" in Fra Luca Pacioli's *Summa*).

37. *Perspectiva Corporum Regularium.* Das ist/ Ein fleyssige Fürweysung Wie die Fünff Regulierten Cörper/ darvon Plato im Timaeo/Unnd Euclides inn sein Elementis schreibt/&c. Durch einen sonderlichen/neuen/behenden und gerechten weg/ der von nie im gebrauch ist gesehen wor-den/ gar Künstlich inn die Perspectiva gebracht/. Und darin ein schöne Anleytung/ wie auss denselbigen Fünff Cörpern one Endt/gar viel andere Cörper/ mancherley Art unnd gestalt/ gemacht/ unnd gefunden werden mügen. Allen Liebhabern der freyen Kunst zu Ehren/ durch Wentzeln Jamnitzer/ burgern und goldtschmid in Nürmberg/ mit Götlicher hülff an tag geben &c. Mit Röm: Kayserlicher May: befreyung/ Inn 15. Jaren nicht nach zudrucken. Anno, M.D.LXVIII. Jamnitzer writes in the preface about optics which he identifies with perspective: "Kunst/welche die alten auff Griegisch OΠTIKHN genent haben/ welche wir sonsten gemeiniglich die Perspective zu nennen pflegen/Nemlich ein Kunst die da lehret/ von eigenschafft/ art und natur/ der Linien und Strom so von unserem gesicht auff andere ding hin und wider geworffen werden/ . . . ." This proves that he had first- or secondhand knowledge of the Italian theoreticians from Alberti to Piero della Francesca. It is obvious that the fourth book of Dürer's *Unterweisung der Messung mit dem Zirkel und Richtscheit* was a main source of his information.

Jamnitzer brings, referring to Plato's Timaeus, the four elements and heaven in relation to the five regular solids.

Fewer.	Tetraedron
Lufft.	Octaedron
Erden.	Hexaedron
Wasser.	Icosaedron
Himel.	Dodecaedron.

As all terrestrial bodies are compounds of the elements, other Geometrica Corpora can be derived from those solids. Jamnitzer brings 140 examples. See also Kepler, *Harmonices Mundi*, Lib. V, Caput I. "De quinque Figuris solidis regularibus."

38. *Astronomia Nova* AITIOΛOΓHTOΣ, *Seu Physica coelestis, tradita commentariis de Motibus Stellae Martis, Ex observationibus G. V. Tychonis Brahe:*

Jussu & sumptibus Rudolphi II. Romanorum Imperatoris & C: Plurium annorum pertinaci studio elaborata. Pragae, A S⁺. C⁺. M.ᵗⁱˢ S⁺. Mathematico Ioanne Keplero. 1619.

39. Cap. LIX. "Demonstratio, quod orbita MARTIS, librati in diametro epicycli, fiat perfecta ellipsis. Et quod area circuli metiatur summam distantiarum ellipticae circumferentiae punctorum."

40. Paris, Louvre.

41. Kepler demonstrated how parabola and hyperbola resulted from the sections of the conus in his *Nova Stereometria Doliorum Vinariorum, in primis Austriaci, figurae ommnium aptissimae.* Lincii, Excudebat Joannes Plancus, sumptibus Authoris. M.DC.XV. "De Sectionibus Coni, solidorum genitricibus." (A German edition was published in the following year with the title *Messe Kunst Archimedis.*) The practical purpose of the work was the measuring of the content of barrels as prescribed by the gauging office in the vine-growing country of Austria. It contains an abundance of geometrical forms and constructions which suggest the formal inventions of the contemporary painters and draughtsmen. They can be traced back in many cases to the geometrical forms developed by Dürer in his *Unterweisung der Messung mit dem Zirkel und Richtscheit* which offered themselves to Kepler as algebraic curves. The stimulating influence of Dürer's book on the development of mathematics in the sixteenth century was immense. Kepler knew and studied Dürer's writings as we may derive from a *passus* in his *Astronomia Nova* and from a letter to David Fabricius. The German language used by Kepler in his *Messe Kunst Archimedis* is seemingly influenced by Dürer.

See the illuminating chapter on Dürer in L. Olschki, *Die Literatur der Technik und der angewandten Wissenschaften vom Mittelalter bis zur Renaissance* (Heidelberg, 1919), pp. 414 ff., and also E. Panofsky, *Albrecht Dürer* (Princeton, 1944), vol. I, p. 255.

42. Compare for the following M. Dvořák, "Ueber Greco und den Manierismus," *Kunstgeschichte als Geistesgeschichte.*

43. *Astronomia Nova* Lib. V, Cap. III, "Summa doctrinae Astronomicae necessaria ad contemplationem Harmoniarum coelestium." Wolf, *A History of Science,* pp. 140–141.

44. *Guilielmi Gilberti, colcestrensis, medici Londinensis, De magnete, magneticisque corporibus, et de magno magnete tellure physiologia nova.* Londini excudebat Petrus Short Anno MDC.

45. Magnetic lines of force, accepting the shape of rays of supernatural light, appear in the Martyrdom of St. Maurice and the Theban Legion which El Greco painted 1581–1584 for the Escorial. The spectral iridescence of El Greco's colors found a congenial framework in the somber, sober, and hermetic Late Renaissance architecture of Juan de Herrera, the very essence of Counter-reformation in building.

Herrera is one of the foremost examples of a scientifically minded artist of the Late Renaissance (A. Ruiz de Arcaute, *J. de Herrera,* Madrid, 1936). His activity in the fields of mathematics, astronomy, and cartography was almost as extensive as in the fine arts. His library consisted mostly of scientific and philosophical works. By 1562 he was entrusted by Honorato Juan with the drawing of the plates for an astronomical treatise by Alfonso el Sabio. He constructed astronomical orbits, astrolabes, equinoctial clocks, and all kinds of mathematical models. The problem of exact location according to longitude and latitude was of particular importance to Spain, with her expansive navigation and her vast colonial empire. In 1573, Herrera received a royal privilege for the use of nautical instruments of his own invention. After the death of Esquivel, he was commissioned to continue the work on the map of Spain.

The demand for increased education in sciences led to the foundation of the Academia de Matemáticas in 1582, an event contemporary with El Greco's work for the Escorial. Herrera was the *spiritus rector* and first director of the new academy, in which mathematics, sciences, military architecture, and philosophy were taught. Herrera was also responsible for the acquisition of a suitable library. In 1584, he ordered from Venice all translations of Copernicus and other works on planetary theories into the *lingua volgare* which were available on the market.

As in the arts a harking back to the Middle Ages is noticeable, so in the philosophy connected with those very exact sciences. The philosophy taught at the Accademia de Matemáticas was particularly the *Ars maior* of Raimundus Lullus. (Also Giordano Bruno lectured on Lullus and his anamnestic method.) The medieval attempt to combine the irrational with highest reason was bound to appeal to the thought of the Late Renaissance. Herrera wrote in those years a *Tratado del Cuerpo Cubico*, an exposition of the *Ars maior* according to the mathematical principles of Euclid and Aristotle.

46. Robert-Dumesnil, *Le Peintre-graveur français*, 11 vols. (Paris, 1835), vol. 5, no. 2.

47. Robert-Dumesnil, vol. 5, no. 34.

48. Berlin, Kupferstichkabinett. J. Q. van Regteren-Altena, *Jacques de Gheyn*, p. 40.

49. *Harmonices Mundi* Liber V Cap. 15.

50. *Ad Vitellionem Paralipomena, Quibus Astronomiae Pars Optica traditur.* . . . Authore Ioanne Keplero, S.C.M. Mathematico. Francofurti, Apud Claudium Marnium & Haeredes Ioannis Aubrii. Anno M.DCIV.

Ioannis Kepleri S.C.M. Mathematici Dioptrice seu Demonstratio eorum quae visui & visibilibus propter Conspicilla non ita pridem inventa accidunt. Augustae Vindelicorum, typis Davidis Franci. M.DCXI.

ADDENDUM TO PAGE 75

An essay by Paul Johansen, published during the war ("Meister Michel Sittow," *Jahrbuch der Preussischen Kunstsammlungen*, vol. 61, 1940, pp. 1 ff.) contains important documentary material about the master. His actual name was Michel Sittow. He was a German, native and citizen of Reval (Talinn) in Estonia, educated in Flanders.

Index

INDEX

Specific works of an artist or author are mentioned in the index only when more than one title is referred to in the text.

1. A. DÜRER: CRUCIFIXION

2. A. DÜRER: PORTRAIT OF HIS MOTHER

4. GERMAN ARTIST OF THE BEGINNING OF THE

3. A. DÜRER: THE SEVEN ANGELS WITH THE

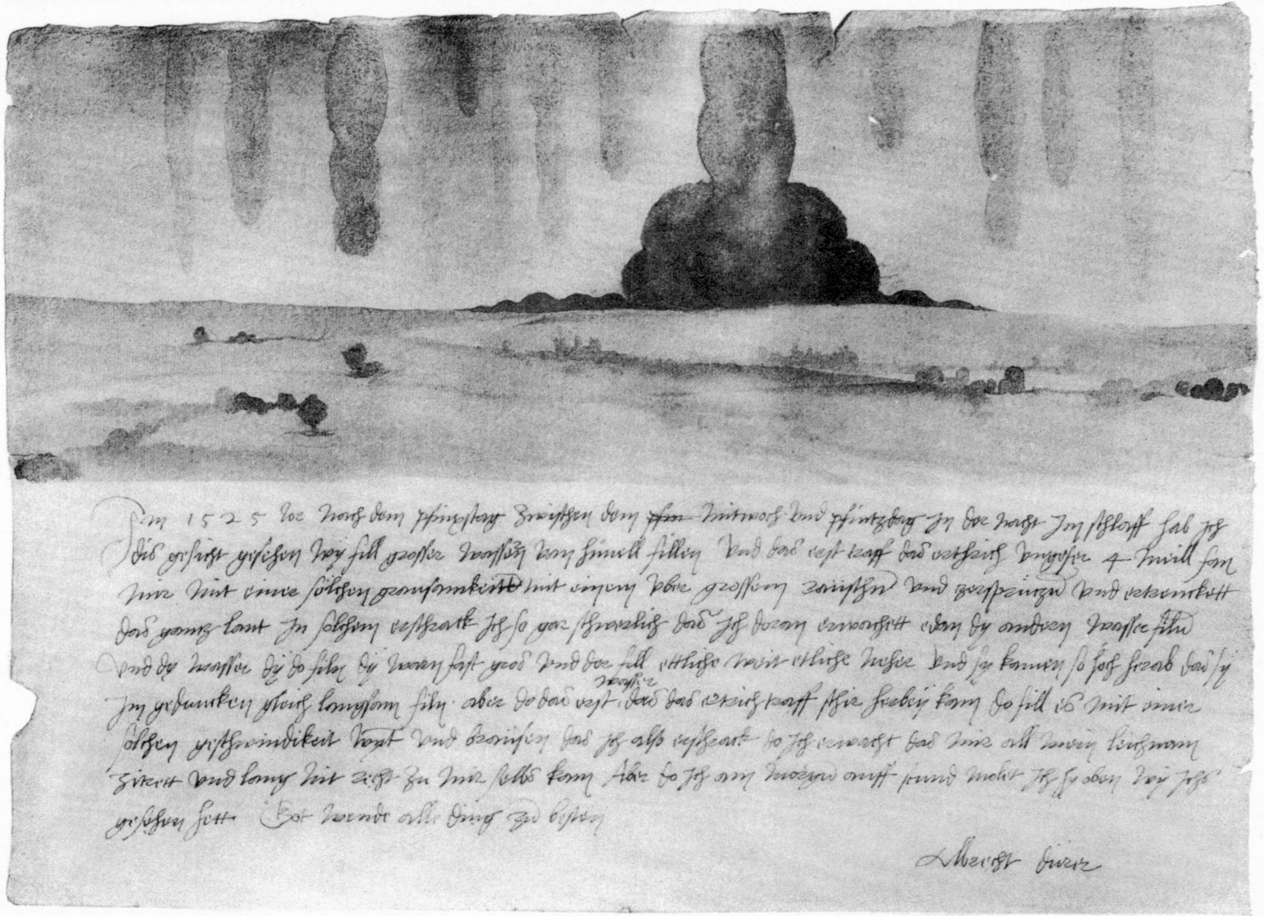

5. A. DÜRER: DREAM VISION

6. A. DÜRER: ARMY BELEAGUERING A CITY

7. A DÜRER: VIEW OF TRENT

8. A. DÜRER: THE ADORATION OF THE TRINITY

9. A. DÜRER: SELF-PORTRAIT AS A JOURNEYMAN

10. A. DÜRER: SELF-PORTRAIT AS THE MAN

11. M. GRÜNEWALD: CRUCIFIXION

12. M. GRÜNEWALD: GLORIFICATION OF MARY

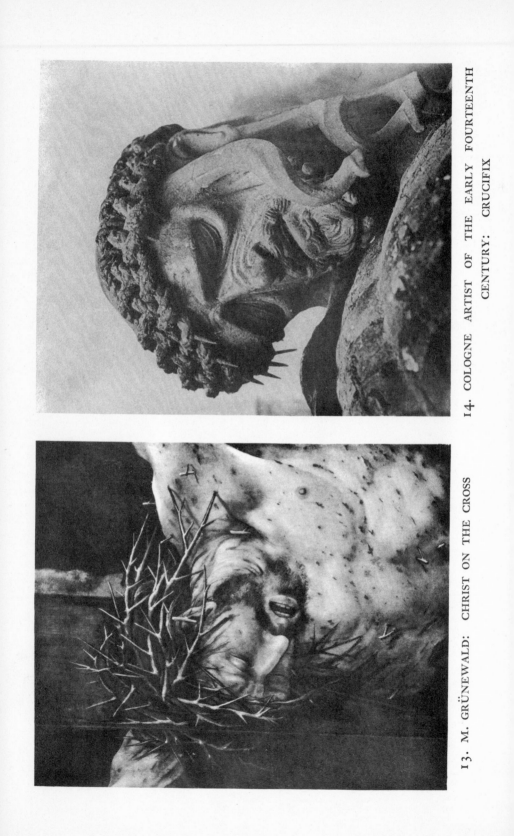

13. M. GRÜNEWALD: CHRIST ON THE CROSS

14. COLOGNE ARTIST OF THE EARLY FOURTEENTH CENTURY: CRUCIFIX

15. M. GRÜNEWALD: ST. DOROTHY

16. M. GRÜNEWALD: THE MADONNA OF STUPPACH

17. M. GRÜNEWALD: THE APOSTLE PETER PROSTRATED

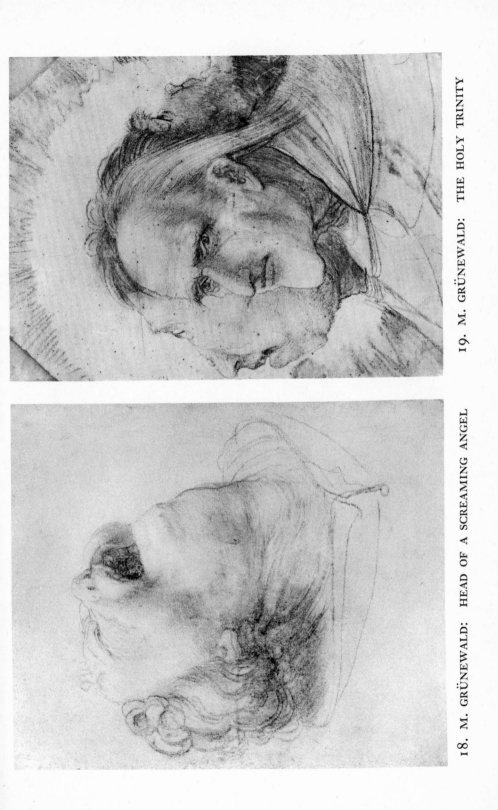

18. M. GRÜNEWALD: HEAD OF A SCREAMING ANGEL

19. M. GRÜNEWALD: THE HOLY TRINITY

20. J. RATGEB: THE RESURRECTION OF CHRIST

21. A. ALTDORFER: FOREST WITH ST. GEORGE AND THE DRAGON

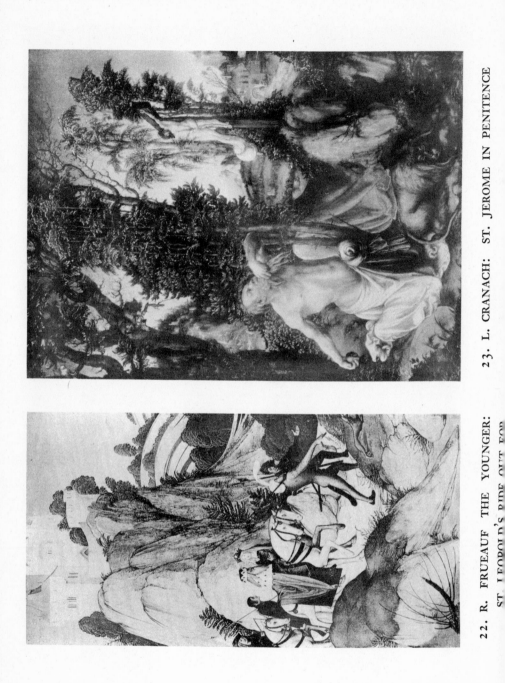

22. R. FRUEAUF THE YOUNGER: ST. LEOPOLD'S PIPE CUT FOR

23. L. CRANACH: ST. JEROME IN PENITENCE

24. A. ALTDORFER: THE WILD MAN'S FAMILY

25. A. ALTDORFER: THE NATIVITY OF CHRIST

26. A. ALTDORFER: ST. JOHN THE EVANGELIST AND ST. JOHN THE BAPTIST

27. A. ALTDORFER: SARMINGSTEIN ON THE DANUBE

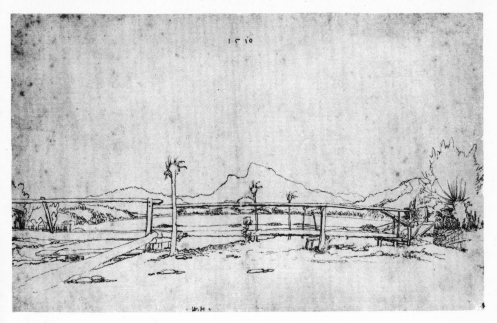

28. W. HUBER: THE MONDSEE IN THE SALZKAMMERGUT

29. A. ALTDORFER: THE BATTLE OF ALEXANDER

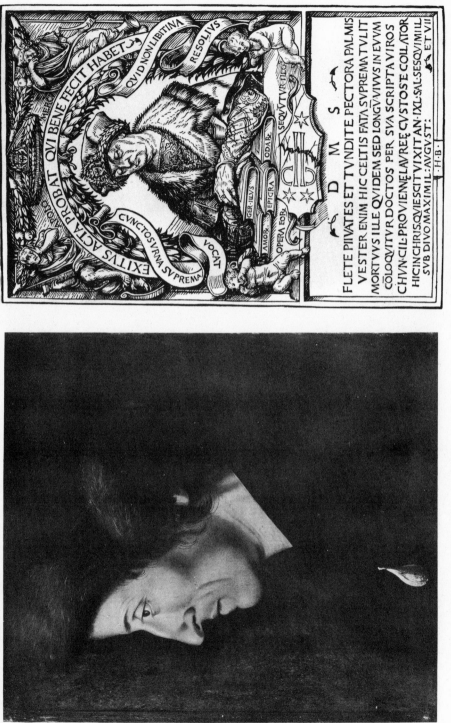

30. H. BURGKMAIR: SEBASTIAN BRANT

31. H. BURGKMAIR: CONRAD CELTES

32. L. CRANACH: JOHANNES CUSPINIAN

33. L. FURTNAGEL: PORTRAIT OF HANS BURGKMAIR
AND HIS WIFE

34. L. CRANACH: FREDERICK THE WISE
PRAYING BEFORE THE MADONNA

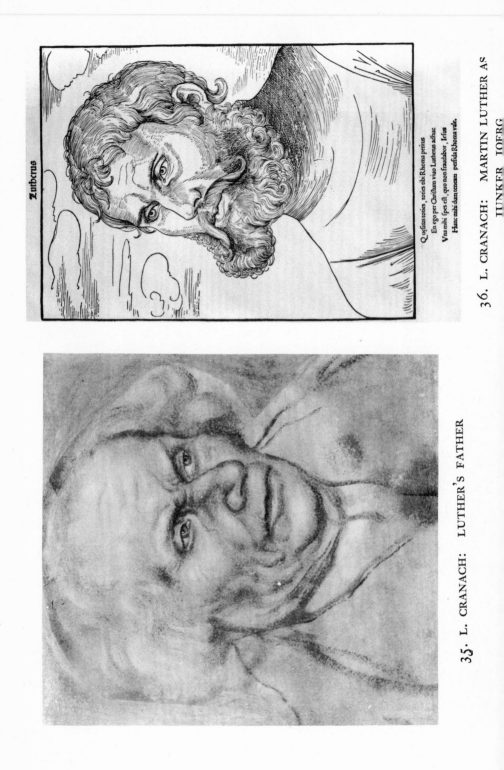

Lutherus

Quefuustonies, totius tibi Rhoma prius
En ego per Chriftum viuo Lutherus adhuc
Vna mihi fpes eft, quo non fraudabor, Iefus
Hunc mihi dum teneam perfida Rhoma vale.

35. L. CRANACH: LUTHER'S FATHER

36. L. CRANACH: MARTIN LUTHER AS
TIUNKER IOERG

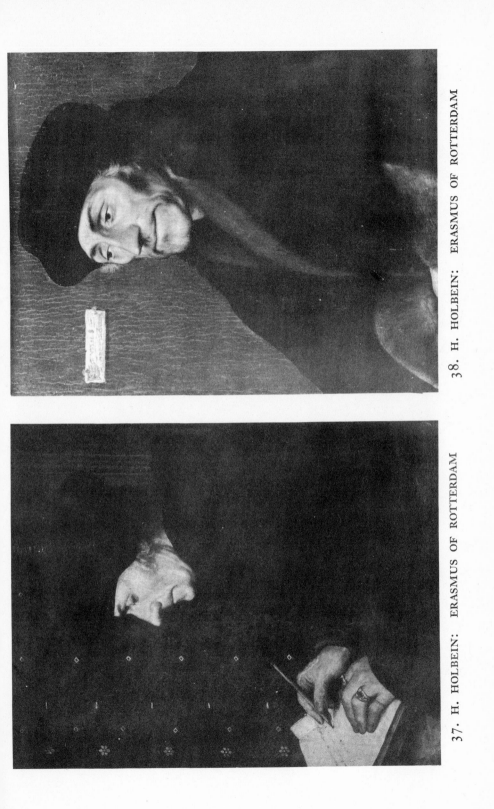

37. H. HOLBEIN: ERASMUS OF ROTTERDAM

38. H. HOLBEIN: ERASMUS OF ROTTERDAM

39. H. HOLBEIN: SIR THOMAS MORE AND HIS FAMILY

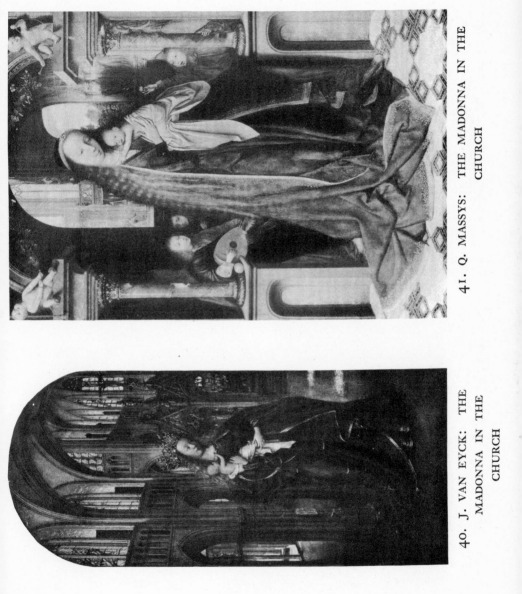

40. J. VAN EYCK: THE MADONNA IN THE CHURCH

41. Q. MASSYS: THE MADONNA IN THE CHURCH

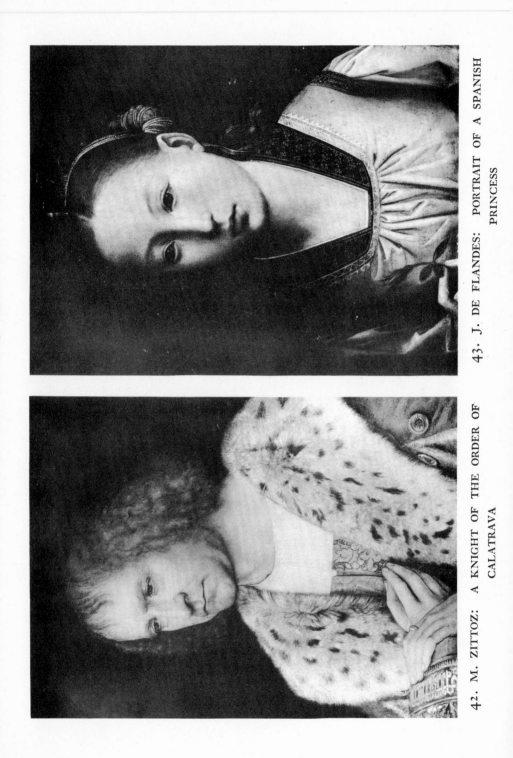

42. M. ZITTOZ: A KNIGHT OF THE ORDER OF CALATRAVA

43. J. DE FLANDES: PORTRAIT OF A SPANISH PRINCESS

44. Q. MASSYS: THE LAMENTATION FOR CHRIST

45. Q. MASSYS: THE HOLY KINDRED

46. J. DE BEER: THE NATIVITY

47. J. GOSSAERT: THE DEATH OF ST. JOHN

48. H. BOSCH: THE CARRYING OF   49. THE MASTER OF THE VIRGO INTER VIRGINES: THE
THE CROSS   THRONE OF MERCY

50. J. DE COCK: ST. CHRISTOPHER

51. L. VAN LEYDEN: SUSANNA BEFORE THE JUDGE

52. P. BRUEGEL: THE BATTLE OF THE ANGELS AND THE DEMONS

53. P. BRUEGEL: PAINTER AND
CONNOISSEUR

54. P. BRUEGEL: THE LARGE FISHES EAT THE LITTLE ONES

55. P. BRUEGEL: THE CONTEST BETWEEN CARNIVAL AND LENT

56. P. BRUEGEL: THE FALL OF ICARUS

57. P. BRUEGEL: THE CENSUS IN BETHLEHEM

58. P. BRUEGEL: THE MONTH OF NOVEMBER

59. IL ROSSO FIORENTINO: THE DEATH OF ADONIS

60. IL ROSSO FIORENTINO: VERTUMNUS AND POMONA

61. FRENCH MASTER OF THE SECOND QUARTER OF THE
SIXTEENTH CENTURY: A GARDEN FESTIVAL

62. SCHOOL OF FONTAINEBLEAU: THE HARVEST AT
FONTAINEBLEAU

63. B. SALOMON: THE TORRENT

LA FONTANA DI ROIAG
IN OVERNIA.

DEO MAGNO AETERNO,
ET BLANDE SCATVRIENTIB. RVBIACIS
NIMPHIS
SVIQ. NOMINIS MEMORIAE PERENNI
GABRIEL SVMEONVS FLOR. EYΔOKIAE
D. S. P. P. C.

64. B. SALOMON: THE FOUNTAIN OF ROIAG

65. F. PRIMATICCIO: DIANA AND ACTAEON

66. F. PRIMATICCIO: THE MASQUERADE OF PERSEPOLIS

67. G. PILON: MATER DOLOROSA

69. J. BELLANGE: THE MARYS AT THE TOMB

68. J. DUVET: THE VISION OF THE CANDLESTICKS

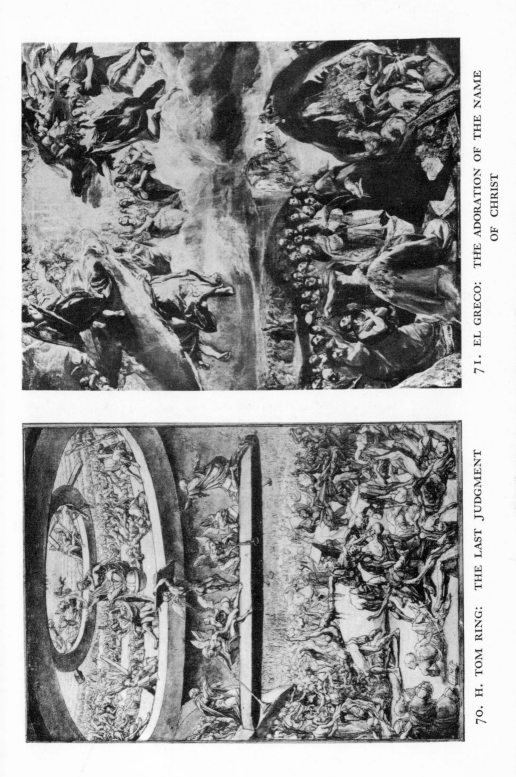

71. EL GRECO: THE ADORATION OF THE NAME
OF CHRIST

70. H. TOM RING: THE LAST JUDGMENT

72. P. BRUEGEL: THE TOWER OF BABEL

73. J. TINTORETTO: THE PARADISE

74. J. TINTORETTO: THE PARADISE

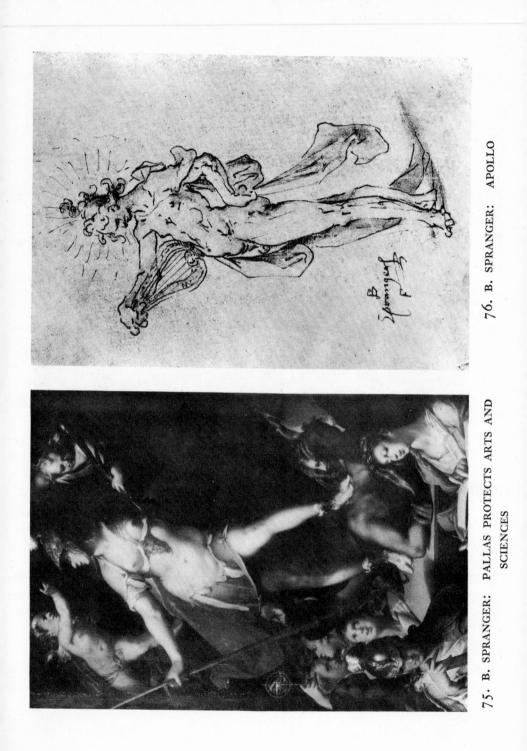

75. B. SPRANGER: PALLAS PROTECTS ARTS AND
SCIENCES

76. B. SPRANGER: APOLLO

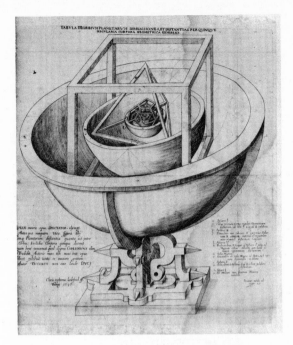

77. J. KEPLER: MYSTERIUM
COSMOGRAPHICUM

78. W. JAMNITZER: PERSPECTIVA CORPORUM REGULARIUM

79. EL GRECO: VIEW OF TOLEDO

80. J. BELLANGE: GROUP OF WOMEN

F180